Easy Crocheted Sweaters

COMPILED BY **Amy Palmer**

⊞ INTERWEAVE.
interweave.com

Contents

*The projects in this collection were
originally published in other Interweave
publications, including* Interweave
Crochet, Interweave Knits, Knitscene,
and PieceWork *magazines. Some have
been altered to update information and/
or conform to space limitations.*

Interweave
A division of F+W Media, Inc.
201 East Fourth Street
Loveland, CO 80537
interweave.com

Manufactured in the United States
by Versa Press

ISBN 978-1-62033-577-2 (pbk.)

Wrinkle Vest

BY TRACY ST. JOHN

The yoke of this lacy vest, worked in a light alpaca blend on a medium hook, curves gently thanks to clever shells of graduated heights. Its seamless top-down construction lets you try it on as you go to adjust the length to your liking. Wear it open or use a shawl pin or ribbon, threaded through the bodice, to close it.

Finished Size

34 (38, 42, 46, 50)" (86.5 [96.5, 106.5, 117, 127] cm) bust circumference. Garment shown measures 34" (86.5 cm), modeled with ½" (1.3 cm) ease.

Yarn

Alpaca with a Twist Socrates (30% baby alpaca, 30% merino, 20% bamboo, 20% nylon; 400 yd [366 m]/3½ oz [100 g]; (**1**)): #3019 Michelle's pink, 2 (2, 3, 3, 3) skeins.

Hook Size

I/9 (5.5 mm) and 7 (4.5 mm). Adjust hook size if necessary to obtain correct gauge.

Notions

Yarn needle; stitch markers (m).

Gauge

4 sh and 8 rows = 4" (10 cm) with larger hook.

Note

* Although garment is seamless, it is made in 3 sections; 2 yoke sections and the main body. The yoke sections are worked horizontally from the middle of the back moving toward the front. Section two of yoke is worked in foundation ch of section one of yoke.

Stitch Guide

Shell (sh): (2 dc, ch 1, 2 dc) in indicated sp.

Picot: Ch 3, sl st in first ch.

Yoke

SECTION ONE

With larger hook, ch 37 (37, 37, 42, 42).
Note: Row 1 beg at neck edge.

Row 1: (RS) Working in 7th ch from hook (counts as hdc and ch 4) work (2 hdc, ch 1, 2 hdc), sk next 4 ch, (2 hdc, ch 1, 2 hdc) in next ch, [sk next 4 ch, sh (see Stitch Guide) in next ch] 2 (2, 2, 3, 3) times, sk next 4 ch, (2 tr, ch 1, 2 tr) in next ch, sk next 4 ch, (3 tr, ch 1, 3 tr) in next ch, sk next 4 ch, tr in last ch, place marker (pm) in top of last tr, turn.

Row 2: Ch 4 (counts as tr), pm in top of tch, (3 tr, ch 1, 3 tr) in next ch-1 sp, (2 tr, ch 1, 2 tr) in next ch-1 sp, sh in each of next 2 (2, 2, 3, 3) ch-1 sps, (2 hdc, ch 1, 2 hdc) in each of next 2 ch-1 sps, hdc in tch, turn.

Row 3: Ch 2 (counts as hdc), (2 hdc, ch 1, 2 hdc) in each of next 2 ch-1 sps, sh in each of next 2 (2, 2, 3, 3) ch-1 sps, (2 tr, ch 1, 2 tr) in next ch-1 sp, (3 tr, ch 1, 3 tr) in next ch-1 sp, tr in tch, pm in top of tr, turn.

Rep Rows 2–3 eleven (twelve, thirteen, fourteen, fifteen) more times. Fasten off.

SECTION TWO

Note: The first row of section two is worked in bottom lps of foundation ch of section one. This becomes the center back of the yoke.

Row 1: With WS of section one facing, join yarn in bottom lp of section one at base of beg hdc (neck edge), ch 2 (counts as hdc), [sk next 4 sts, (2 hdc, ch 1, 2 hdc) in next st] 2 times, [sk next 4 sts, sh in next st] 2 (2, 2, 3, 3) times, sk next 4 sts, (2 tr, ch 1, 2 tr) in next st, sk next 4 sts, (3 tr, ch 1, 3 tr) in next st, sk next 4 sts, tr in last st, pm in top of last tr, turn.

Rows 2–3: Rep Rows 2–3 of yoke section one.

Rep Rows 2–3 eleven (twelve, thirteen, fourteen, fifteen) more times. Do not fasten off.

MAIN BODY

Rotate work 90 degrees. Beg working along length of yoke, working sh in each marked st, removing m as you go.

Row 1: (RS) Ch 3 (counts as dc through-out), dc in first st, sh in next 24 (26, 28, 30, 32) marked sts, sh in foundation ch at center back of yoke, sh in next 24 (26, 28, 30, 32) marked sts, 2 dc in last marked st, turn—49 (53, 57, 61, 65) sh.

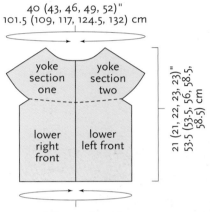

40 (43, 46, 49, 52)"
101.5 (109, 117, 124.5, 132) cm

21 (21, 22, 23, 23)"
53.5 (53.5, 56, 58.5, 58.5) cm

34 (38, 42, 46, 50)"
86.5 (96.5, 106.5, 117, 127) cm

DIVIDE FOR FRONTS AND BACK

Row 2: (make armholes) Ch 3, dc in first dc, sh in next 7 (8, 9, 10, 11) ch-1 sps, *ch 10 (10, 10, 15, 15), sk next 10 sh**, sh in next 15 (17, 19, 21, 23) ch-1 sps; rep from * to **, sh in next 7 (8, 9, 10, 11) ch-1 sps, 2 dc in last dc, turn—29 (33, 37, 41, 45) sh.

Row 3: Ch 3, dc in same dc, sh in next 7 (8, 9, 10, 11) ch-1 sps, *sk next 2 ch, sh in next ch, [sk next 4 ch, sh in next ch] 1 (1, 1, 2, 2) times, sk next 2 ch**, sh in next 15 (17, 19, 21, 23) ch-1 sps; rep from * to **, sh in next 7 (8, 9, 10, 11) ch-1 sps, 2 dc in last dc, turn—33 (37, 41, 47, 51) sh.

Row 4: Ch 3, dc in first dc, sh in each ch-1 sp to last dc, 2 dc in last dc, turn—33 (37, 41, 47, 51) sh.

Rep Row 4 nineteen (nineteen, twenty, twenty-one, twenty-one) times or to desired length to hip, ending with a RS row. Do not fasten off.

EDGING

Rotate work 90 degrees. *Note: Beg edging vest, working up right front, cont along neck edge, down left front, and around bottom edge, ending at right-front corner.* With smaller hook, ch 1, 3 sc in same st (corner made), cont as described above in evenly spaced sc, working a picot (see Stitch Guide) every 4 sts, and working 3 sc in each corner to beg sc, sl st in beg sc to join. Fasten off.

ARMHOLE EDGING

With RS facing, work as for body edging, joining yarn at center underarm and working around each armhole. Weave in ends and block to measurements. 🍃

TRACY ST. JOHN'S ideal world would let her crochet 24 hours a day. She could get 43,200 double crochets done every day. King-size afghans for everyone on her Christmas list!

Yoke Pattern

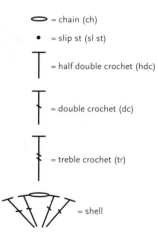

◯ = chain (ch)

• = slip st (sl st)

| = half double crochet (hdc)

† = double crochet (dc)

‡ = treble crochet (tr)

= shell

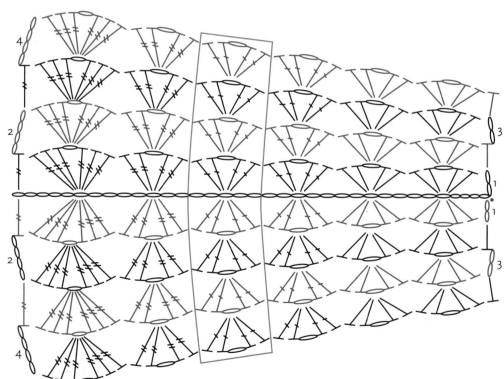

Russel Sweater

BY ANNETTE PETAVY

Sized for all the men in your life—with three boys' sizes and three men's sizes—this sweater is both rugged and stylish. It is worked cuff to cuff first in back-loop-only half double crochet, and then the body is picked up and worked downward in front-loop-only single crochet.

Finished Size

27½ (29, 30, 38, 41, 44½)" (70 [73.5, 76, 96.5, 104, 113] cm) chest circumference. Garment shown measures 41" (96.5 cm), modeled with 5" (12.5 cm) ease.

Yarn

Lion Brand Superwash Merino (100% merino; 306 yd [280 m]/3½ oz [100 g]; (3)): #108 denim, 3 (3, 4, 6, 6, 7) balls.

Hook

Sizes 7 (4.5 mm) and H/8 (5 mm). Adjust hook size if necessary to obtain correct gauge.

Notions

Stitch markers (m); yarn needle.

Gauge

19 sts = 4" (10 cm) in hdc blo with smaller hook; 16 rows = 5" (12.5 cm) in hdc blo with smaller hook, unstretched; 17 sts and 18 rows = 4" (10 cm) in sc flo with larger hook, stretched.

Notes

* Garment yoke is worked cuff to cuff in a single piece for both back and front.

* Bottom of the garment is worked from the yoke down, back and front separately.

* Turning chain (tch) does not count as st throughout.

* For yoke, ch 1 for turning ch. If edge pulls in, try ch 2.

* Sl sts in beg of rows and sts left unworked at end of row are dec and do not count in st count.

* Yoke and sleeves will stretch when sweater is worn, making final sleeve length slightly longer than indicated in pattern.

Stitch Guide

Foundation Half Double Crochet (fhdc): Ch 3, yarn over, insert hook in 3rd chain from hook, yarn over and pull up loop (3 loops on hook), yarn over and draw through 1 loop (1 chain made), yarn over and draw through all loops on hook—1 foundation half double crochet. *Yarn over, insert hook under the 2 loops of the "chain" stitch of last stitch and pull up loop, yarn over and draw through 1 loop, yarn over and draw through all loops on hook; repeat from * for length of foundation.

Inc: Work 2 sts in indicated st.

Sweater

RIGHT SLEEVE

With smaller hook, ch 35 (35, 37, 41, 43, 45).

Set-up row: (WS) Ch 1 (does not count as a st throughout), hdc in 2nd ch from hook and in each ch across—35 (35, 37, 41, 43, 45) sts.

Row 1: (RS) Inc (see Stitch Guide) in first st, hdc blo in each st to last st, inc in last st, place marker (pm) to indicate RS—2 sts inc'd.

Cont in hdc blo, rep Row 1 every 2nd row 1 (3, 3, 8, 16, 25) more times—39 (43, 45, 59, 77, 97) sts. Rep Row 1 every 3rd row 12 (12, 13, 16, 11, 5) times—63 (67, 71, 91, 99, 107) sts. Cont even in hdc blo until work measures 13½ (14½, 16¼, 22, 22, 22)" (34.5 [37, 41.5, 56, 56, 56] cm). Pm at each edge to mark end of sleeve. Count number of rows worked since last inc; this is number A.

YOKE

Cont working even in hdc blo until work measures 17¼ (18¾, 20¾, 28¼, 29, 30)" (44 [47.5, 52.5, 72, 73.5, 76] cm) ending with WS row. Pm in center st of row—31 (33, 35, 45, 49, 53) sts each for back and front plus 1 center st at shoulder. Count number of rows worked since end of sleeve; this is number B.

SHAPE FRONT NECK

Row 1: (RS) Hdc blo to 5 sts before m, turn leaving rem sts unworked—26 (28, 30, 40, 44, 48) sts for front.

Row 2: Sl st in first 3 (3, 4, 4, 4, 4) sts, ch 1 (does not count as st throughout), hdc blo to end, turn—23 (25, 26, 36, 40, 44) sts.

Row 3: Hdc blo to last 1 (2, 2, 2, 2, 3) hdc, turn leaving rem sts unworked—22 (23, 24, 34, 38, 41) sts.

Row 4: Ch 1, hdc2tog (see Glossary) blo, hdc blo to end—21 (22, 23, 33, 37, 40) sts.

Row 5: Hdc blo to last 2 sts, hdc2tog blo, turn—20 (21, 22, 32, 36, 39) sts.

Sizes 38 (41, 44½)" only

Rep Rows 4–5—20 (21, 22, 30, 34, 37) sts.

All sizes

Work 5 (7, 7, 7, 7, 9) rows even in hdc blo.

SHAPE NECK

Sizes 38 (41, 44½)" only

Row 1: (RS) Hdc blo to last st, inc in last st—31 (35, 38) sts.

Row 2: Inc in first st, hdc blo to end—32 (36, 39) sts.

All sizes

Row 3: Hdc blo to last st, inc in last st—21 (22, 23, 33, 37, 40) sts.

Row 4: Inc in first st, hdc blo to end—22 (23, 24, 34, 38, 41) sts.

Row 5: Hdc blo across, fhdc (see Glossary) 1 (2, 2, 2, 2, 3), turn—23 (25, 26, 36, 40, 44) sts.

Row 6: Ch 4 (4, 5, 5, 5, 5), hdc in 2nd ch from hook and in each ch, hdc blo to end—26 (28, 30, 40, 44, 48) sts.

Row 7: Hdc blo across, fhdc 8 (8, 8, 9, 9, 9)—34 (36, 38, 49, 53, 57) sts.

Do not fasten off.

SHAPE BACK NECK

With RS facing, a separate ball of yarn, and working in first row of front-neck shaping, sk 2 (2, 2, 3, 3, 3) sts after shoulder m, join yarn with hdc blo in next st, hdc blo to end—29 (31, 33, 42, 46, 50) sts. Work even in hdc blo for 17 (19, 19, 21, 21, 23) rows ending with WS row. Fasten off. Replace hook in live st at front neck. (RS) Hdc in last worked st of back neck, hdc blo to end—63 (67, 71, 91, 99, 107) sts. Work even in hdc blo for number B rows. Pm at each edge to mark beg of sleeve.

LEFT SLEEVE

Work even even in hdc for number A rows.

Row 1: Cont in patt hdc2tog at beg and end of row—61 (65, 69, 89, 97, 105) sts.

Cont in patt, rep Row 1 every 3rd row 11 (11, 12, 15, 10, 4) times—39 (43, 45, 59, 77, 97) sts. Work 1 row even in hdc blo. Rep Row 1 every 2nd row 2 (4, 4, 9, 17, 26) times—35 (35, 37, 41, 43, 45) sts.

Next row: Hdc blo across. Work even if necessary until sleeve measures 13½ (14½, 16¼, 22, 22, 22)" (34.5 [37, 41.5, 56, 56, 56] cm) from sleeve m. Fasten off.

LOWER BACK

With larger hook, RS facing, join yarn at left sleeve m and work 58 (62, 66, 83, 92, 101) sc across back sts, to right sleeve m.

Row 1: Ch 1 (does not count as a st), sc flo across.

Rep row 1 until lower back measures 9 (11½, 13½, 15, 15¾, 15¼" (23 [29, 34.5, 38, 40, 38.5] cm) ending with a RS row. Fasten off.

LOWER FRONT

Work as for lower back.

Finishing

Block pieces to measurements. Weave in loose ends. When weaving in loose end at neck, close small gap front/back neckline join. Sew sleeve seams and side seams. With smaller hook, work 1 row of sc around neck. 🖊

From her home near Lyon, France, ANNETTE PETAVY maintains a website atannettepetavy.com. Visit her site for blog updates, unique patterns, and crochet kits. When not crocheting or hammering on her computer, Annette is most often found in her kitchen or garden.

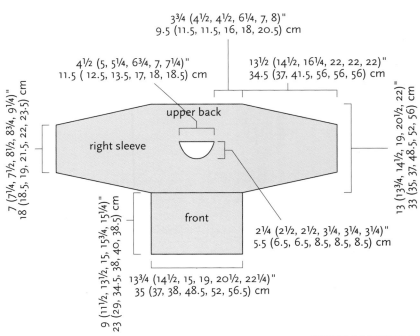

3¾ (4½, 4½, 6¼, 7, 8)"
9.5 (11.5, 11.5, 16, 18, 20.5) cm

4½ (5, 5¼, 6¾, 7, 7¼)"
11.5 (12.5, 13.5, 17, 18, 18.5) cm

13½ (14½, 16¼, 22, 22, 22)"
34.5 (37, 41.5, 56, 56, 56) cm

13 (13¾, 14½, 19, 20½, 22)"
33 (35, 37, 48.5, 52, 56) cm

upper back

right sleeve

7 (7¼, 7½, 8½, 8¾, 9¼)"
18 (18.5, 19, 21.5, 22, 23.5) cm

front

2¼ (2½, 2½, 3¼, 3¼, 3¼)"
5.5 (6.5, 6.5, 8.5, 8.5, 8.5) cm

9 (11½, 13½, 15, 15¾, 15¼)"
23 (29, 34.5, 38, 40, 38.5) cm

13¾ (14½, 15, 19, 20½, 22¼)"
35 (37, 38, 48.5, 52, 56.5) cm

Wool Bam Boo Cardigan

BY KRISTEN TENDYKE

Tunisian knit stitch creates a fabric that's denser and less stretchy than fabric knitted with stockinette stitch. This simple technique combined with full-fashion shaping creates a warm, form-flattering cardigan. Lace trim at the cuffs and hem add a feminine touch.

Finished Size

30 (34, 38, 42, 46)" (76 [86.5, 96.5, 106.5, 117] cm) bust circumference, buttoned. Cardigan shown measures 34" (86.5 cm).

Yarn

Classic Elite Wool Bam Boo (50% wool, 50% bamboo; 118 yd [108 m]/1¾ oz [50 g]; (3)): #1648, denim blue, 14 (15, 17, 19, 21) balls.

Hook Size

G/6 (4 mm) 22" (56 cm) long flexible Afghan (Tunisian) hook and size E/4 (3.5 mm). Adjust hook sizes if necessary to obtain the correct gauge.

Notions

Yarn needle; seven ½" (1.3 cm) buttons; removable marker (m).

Gauge

23 sts and 22 rows = 4" (10 cm) in Tunisian knit stitch on larger hook. The row gauge consists of forward pass and return pass counted as 1 row. Be sure to wash your swatch.

Stitch Guide

Tunisian Knit (Tks; see page 12)
Foundation Forward Pass (FwdP): Insert hook through the ridge lp on the backside of the 2nd ch, yo, pull up a lp, leave lp on hook, pull up a lp through ridge lp in each ch across (first lp counts as first st).

Foundation Return Pass (RetP): Yo and pull through first lp on hook (1 ch made), *yo, draw through 2 lps on hook; rep from * until 1 lp rem; do not turn.

Row 1 Forward Pass (FwdP): Pull up a lp in each stitch across as foll: Beg with 2nd st (existing lp counts as first st) *insert bet next vertical bars under horizontal strands, yo, draw up a lp, leave lp on hook; rep from * in each st across.

Row 1 Return Pass (RetP): Work as for Foundation RetP.

Rep Row 1 FwdP and RetP for patt (counts as 1 row).

Right-Slant Dec (RSdec): Sk next st, insert hook in next st, pull forward the back lp, insert hook in skipped st, yo and draw through lp.

Left-Slant Dec (LSdec): Insert hook in next st, pull forward front lp, insert hook in next st, yo and draw through lp.

Make 1 Inc (M1): Insert hook between next 2 sts, draw up a lp.

Picot Edge (multiple of 3 sts)
*Sl st in the next st, ch 2, sl st in same st, sl st in next st; rep from * across.

Notes

* When working Tunisian knit stitch, do not turn the work; all work is done on the RS

SHAPE ARMHOLES

Row 1 FwdP: Join yarn with sl st to 6th st from beg of row, work first Tks in 6th st, Tks to last 5 sts; RetP work even—76 (88, 99, 111, 122) sts.

Row 2 FwdP: (dec row) Tks in next st (2 lps on hook), RSdec, Tks to last 4 sts, LSdec, Tks in rem 2 sts; RetP work even—74 (86, 97, 109, 120) sts.

Row 3: Tks across.

Rep Rows 2–3 zero (three, five, five, five) more times—74 (82, 89, 101, 110) sts, then work Row 2 zero (one, two, four, seven) more times—74 (78, 83, 91, 96) sts. Work even until armhole measures 7¼ (7¾, 8¼, 8¾, 9¼)" (18.5 [19.5, 21, 22.25, 23.5] cm) from beg of shaping, end with RetP completed.

SHAPE NECK AND RIGHT SHOULDER

Note: Unworked sts will remain on hook until last row.

Row 1 FwdP: 1 lp on hook (counts as st here and throughout), Tks in next 28 (30, 31, 33, 35) sts; work RetP for 26 (28, 29, 30, 32) sts.

Row 2 FwdP: Tks in next 20 (22, 23, 24, 26) sts; RetP 18 (20, 21, 21, 23) sts.

Row 3 FwdP: Tks in next 14 (16, 17, 17, 19) sts; RetP 12 (14, 15, 15, 16) sts.

Row 4 FwdP: Tks in next 9 (11, 12, 12, 13) sts; RetP 8 (9, 10, 10, 10) sts.

Row 5 FwdP: Tks in next 5 (6, 7, 7, 7) sts; RetP 4 (4, 5, 5, 5) sts.

BEG LEFT SHOULDER

Row 6 FwdP: Work across row to last 3 (3, 3, 4, 4) sts; RetP 21 (23, 24, 25, 27) sts.

Row 7 FwdP: Tks in next 17 (19, 20, 20, 22) sts; RetP 15 (17, 18, 18, 20) sts.

Row 8 FwdP: Tks in next 11 (13, 14, 14, 15) sts; RetP 10 (12, 13, 13, 14) sts.

Row 9 FwdP: Tks in next 7 (8, 9, 9, 9) sts; RetP 6 (7, 8, 8, 8) sts.

Row 10 FwdP: Tks in next 3 (3, 4, 4, 4) sts; RetP 2 (2, 3, 3, 3) sts.

Row 11 FwdP: Tks to end of row; work RetP even on all sts. Fasten off.

Back

With larger hook, ch 86 (98, 109, 121, 132).

Work Foundation FwdP and RetP (see Stitch Guide) across ch—86 (98, 109, 121, 132) sts. Work Row 1 FwdP and RetP (see Stitch Guide) even for 2 rows, end with RetP completed.

SHAPE WAIST

Row 1 FwdP: (dec row) *Tks (see Stitch Guide) in next st (2 lps on hook), RSdec (see Stitch Guide), Tks to last 4 sts, LSdec (see Stitch Guide), Tks rem 2 sts; RetP work even—84 (96, 107, 119, 130) sts. Work even in Tks for 2 (3, 4, 5, 5) more rows, end with RetP completed; rep from * 3 more times—78 (90, 101, 113, 124) sts.

Next row: (inc row) Tks in next st (2 lps on hook), M1 (see Stitch Guide), Tks to last 2 sts, M1, Tks in rem 2 sts; RetP work even—80 (92, 103, 115, 126) sts. Work 9 rows even, end with RetP completed; rep from * 3 more times—86 (98, 109, 121, 132) sts. Tks even until piece measures 10½ (11, 11½, 12, 12½)" (26.5 [28, 29, 30.5, 31.5] cm) from beg, end with RetP completed. Fasten off.

Left Front

With larger hook, ch 43 (49, 55, 60, 66). Work Tks Foundation FwdP and RetP across ch—43 (49, 55, 60, 66) sts. Work even in Tks for two rows, ending with RetP completed.

SHAPE WAIST

Row 1 FwdP: (dec row) Tks in next st (2 lps on hook) work RSdec, Tks to end; RetP work even—42 (48, 54, 59, 65) sts.

Work even in Tks for 2 (3, 4, 5, 5) rows; rep from * 3 more times—39 (45, 51, 56, 62) sts.

Next Row FwdP: (inc row) Tks in next st (2 lps on hook), M1, Tks to end of row; work RetP even—40 (46, 52, 57, 63) sts. Work 9 rows even; rep from * 3 more times—43 (49, 55, 60, 66) sts. Work even until piece measures 10½ (11, 11½, 12, 12½)" (26.5 [28, 29, 30.5, 31.5] cm) from beg, end with RetP completed. Fasten off.

SHAPE ARMHOLES

Row 1 FwdP: Join yarn with sl st to 6th st from beg of row, work first Tks in 6th st, Tks across row; work RetP even—38 (44, 50, 55, 61) sts.

Row 2 FwdP: (dec row) Tks in next st (2 lps on hook), RSdec, Tks to end; RetP work even—37 (43, 49, 54, 60) sts.

Row 3: Work even in Tks.

Rep Rows 2–3 zero (three, five, five, five) more times—37 (40, 44, 49, 55) sts, then work Row 2 zero (one, two, four, seven) time(s)—37 (39, 42, 45, 48) sts. Work even until armhole measures 4½ (5, 5½, 6, 6½)" (11.5 [12.5, 14, 15, 16.5] cm) from beg of shaping, end with RetP completed.

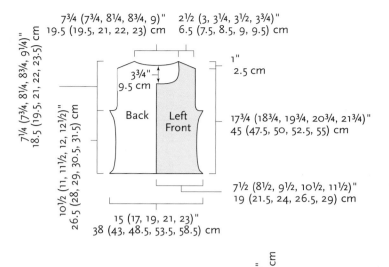

7¾ (7¾, 8¼, 8¾, 9)"
19.5 (19.5, 21, 22, 23) cm

2½ (3, 3¼, 3½, 3¾)"
6.5 (7.5, 8.5, 9, 9.5) cm

7¼ (7¾, 8¼, 8¾, 9¼)"
18.5 (19.5, 21, 22, 23.5) cm

3¾"
9.5 cm

1"
2.5 cm

Back

Left Front

10½ (11, 11½, 12, 12½)"
26.5 (28, 29, 30.5, 31.5) cm

17¾ (18¾, 19¾, 20¾, 21¾)"
45 (47.5, 50, 52.5, 55) cm

7½ (8½, 9½, 10½, 11½)"
19 (21.5, 24, 26.5, 29) cm

15 (17, 19, 21, 23)"
38 (43, 48.5, 53.5, 58.5) cm

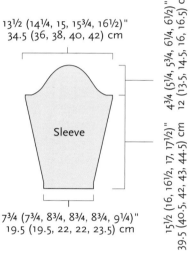

13½ (14¼, 15, 15¾, 16½)"
34.5 (36, 38, 40, 42) cm

4¾ (5¼, 5¾, 6¼, 6½)"
12 (13.5, 14.5, 16, 16.5) cm

Sleeve

15½ (16, 16½, 17, 17½)"
39.5 (40.5, 42, 43, 44.5) cm

7¾ (7¾, 8¾, 8¾, 8¾, 9¼)"
19.5 (19.5, 22, 22, 23.5) cm

Tunisian Knit Stitch

Tunisian knit stitch (Tks) is a variation of Tunisian crochet that mimics the look of knitted stockinette stitch. Tunisian crochet is made using a very long crochet hook. Each row is worked in two steps—a forward pass and a return pass—without turning; the RS is always facing.

Start with a foundation ch equal to the number of sts required, turn.

Foundation Forward Pass: Insert hook in 2nd ch from hook, yo, pull up a lp, leaving lp on hook, *insert hook in next ch, yo, pull up a lp, leaving lp on hook; rep from * to end of row. There is one lp on hook for every ch. Do not turn work.

Foundation Return Pass: Ch 1, *yo, draw through first 2 lps on hook (**FIGURE 1**); rep from * to end of row, 1 lp rem on hook. This lp counts as first st of next row.

Row 1, Forward Pass: Sk first vertical bars, *insert hook between next vertical bars under horizontal strands (**FIGURE 2**), yo, pull up a lp, leaving lp on hook; rep from * to end of row. There is one lp on hook for every st. Do not turn work.

Row 1, Return Pass: Rep as for Foundation Return Pass (**FIGURE 3**).

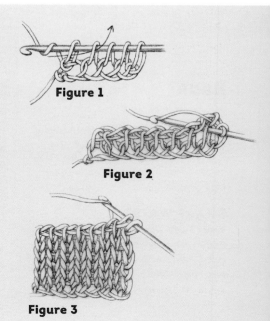

Figure 1

Figure 2

Figure 3

SHAPE NECK

Row 1 FwdP: Tks to last 8 (8, 7, 7, 7) sts; work RetP even—29 (31, 35, 38, 41) sts.

Row 2 FwdP: Tks 27 (29, 32, 35, 38) sts (includes beg lp here and throughout this section); work RetP even.

Row 3 FwdP: Tks 25 (27, 29, 32, 35) sts; work RetP even.

Row 4 FwdP: Tks 23 (25, 26, 29, 32) sts; work RetP even.

Row 5 FwdP: (Dec) Tks to last 4 sts, work LSdec, Tks to end; work RetP even—22 (24, 25, 28, 31) sts.

Rep Row 5 four (four, four, six, three) more times—18 (20, 21, 22, 28) sts.

Next row: Work even in Tks.

Next row FwdP: (dec row) Tks to last 4 sts, work LSdec, Tks to end; work RetP even.

Next row: Work even in Tks. Work last two rows 3 (3, 3, 2, 6) more times. Work even until armhole measures same as back to shoulder shaping.

SHAPE SHOULDER

Note: Unworked sts will rem on hook until last row.

Row 1 FwdP: Tks 14 (16, 17, 19, 21) sts (includes lp at beg of row here and throughout); RetP work 12 (14, 15, 16, 18) sts.

Row 2 FwdP: Tks 12 (14, 15, 16, 18) sts; RetP work 9 (11, 12, 12, 14) sts.

Row 3 FwdP: Tks 9 (11, 12, 12, 14) sts; RetP work 6 (8, 9, 9, 10) sts.

Row 4 FwdP: Tks 6 (8, 9, 9, 10); RetP work 4 (5, 6, 6, 6) sts.

Row 5 FwdP: Tks 4 (5, 6, 6, 6); RetP work 2 (2, 3, 3, 3) sts.

Row 6 FwdP: Tks 2 (2, 3, 3, 3) sts; RetP work even across all sts on hook. Fasten off.

Right Front

With larger hook, ch 43 (49, 55, 60, 66).

Work Tks Foundation FwdP and RetP across ch—43 (49, 55, 60, 66) sts. Work even for 2 rows, end with RetP completed.

SHAPE WAIST

Row 1 FwdP: (dec row) Tks to last 4 sts, work LSdec, Tks to end; RetP work even—42 (48, 54, 59, 65) sts.

Work even for 2 (3, 4, 5, 5) rows; work last 3 (4, 5, 6, 6) rows 3 more times—39 (45, 51, 56, 62) sts.

Next Row: (inc row) Tks to last 2 sts, M1, Tks to end; work RetP even. Work 9 rows even. Work last 10 rows 3 more times—43 (49, 55, 60, 66) sts. Work even until piece measures 10½ (11, 11½, 12, 12½)" (26.5 [28, 29, 30.5, 31.5] cm), end with RetP completed.

SHAPE ARMHOLES

Row 1 FwdP: Tks to last 5 sts; work RetP even—38 (44, 50, 55, 61) sts.

Row 2 FwdP: (dec row) Tks to last 4 sts, LSdec, Tks to end; RetP work even—37 (43, 49, 54, 60) sts.

Row 3: Work even in Tks.

Rep Rows 2–3 zero (three, five, five, five) more times—37 (40, 44, 49, 55) sts, then work Row 2 zero (one, two, four, seven) time(s)—37 (39, 42, 45, 48) sts. Work even until armhole measures 4½ (5, 5½, 6, 6½)" (11.5 [12.5, 14, 15, 16.5] cm) from beg of shaping, end with RetP completed.

SHAPE NECK

Row 1 FwdP: Join yarn with sl st to the 9th (9th, 8th, 8th, 8th) st, work first Tks st in same st, Tks to end; RetP work even—29 (31, 35, 38, 41). Fasten off.

Row 2 FwdP: Join yarn with sl st to 3rd (3rd, 4th, 4th, 4th) st, work first st in same st, Tks to end; RetP work even—27 (29, 32, 35, 38) sts. Fasten off.

Rows 3–4: Rep Row 2—23 (25, 26, 29, 32) sts.

Row 5 FwdP: (dec row) Tks next st (2 lps on hook), work RSdec, Tks to end; RetP work even—22 (24, 25, 28, 31) sts.

Rep Row 5 four (four, four, six, three) more times—18 (20, 21, 22, 28) sts.

Next row: Work even in Tks.

Next row: (dec row) Tks next st (2 lps on hook), work RSdec, Tks to end; RetP work even.

Next row: Work even in Tks. Rep last 2 rows 3 (3, 3, 2, 6) more times—14 (16, 17, 19, 21) sts. Work even until armhole measures same as back to shoulder shaping.

SHAPE SHOULDER

Row 1 FwdP: Tks in next 12 (14, 15, 16, 18) sts (includes first lp on hook here and throughout); RetP work even.

Row 2 FwdP: Tks in next 9 (11, 12, 12, 14) sts; work RetP even.

Row 3 FwdP: Tks in next 6 (8, 9, 9, 10) sts; work RetP even.

Row 4 FwdP: Tks in next 4 (5, 6, 6, 6) sts; work RetP even.

Row 5 FwdP: Tks in next 2 (2, 3, 3, 3) sts; work RetP even.

Row 6 FwdP and RetP: Work even. Fasten off.

SLEEVES

With larger hook, ch 44 (44, 50, 50, 54). Work Tks Foundation FwdP and RetP across ch—44 (44, 50, 50, 54) sts. Work even for 2 rows, end with RetP completed.

SHAPE SLEEVE

Row 1 FwdP: (inc row) Tks in next st (2 lps on hook), M1, Tks across row to last 2 sts, M1, Tks to end; RetP work even—46 (46, 52, 52, 56) sts.

Rows 2 and 3: Work even.

Rep Rows 1–3 four (eleven, four, eleven, five) more times—54 (60, 68, 74, 66) sts. Cont in Tks across all sts working Row 1

every 5th row 12 (7, 13, 8, 14) times—78 (82, 86, 90, 94) sts. Work even until piece measures 15½ (16, 16½, 17, 17½)" (39.5 [40.5, 42, 43, 44.5] cm) from beg, end with RetP completed. Fasten off.

SHAPE CAP

Row 1 FwdP: Join yarn with sl st to 6th st from beg of row, work first Tks st in same st, Tks across to last 5 sts; RetP work even—68 (72, 76, 80, 84) sts rem.

Row 2 FwdP: (dec row) Tks next st (2 lps on hook), work RSdec, Tks to last 4 sts, work LSdec, Tks to end; RetP work even—66 (70, 74, 78, 82) sts.

Row 3: Work even.

Rep Rows 2–3 two (two, four, four, four) more times—62 (66, 66, 70, 74) sts, then work Row 2 only 20 (22, 22, 24, 26) times, end with RetP completed—22 sts rem. Fasten off.

Next row FwdP: Join yarn with sl st to 5th st from beg of row, work first Tks in same st, Tks in next 13 sts; RetP work even—14 sts. Fasten off.

Finishing

Block pieces to measurements. Sew shoulder seams and side seams.

SLEEVE TRIM

With smaller hook and RS facing, join yarn with sl st to right edge of sleeve lower edge.

Row 1: Ch 1 (counts as first sc) work 42 (42, 50, 50, 58) sc across, turn—43 (43, 51, 51, 59) sc.

Row 2: Ch 1, sc in first sc, ch 3 (counts as dc, ch 1), sk next sc, dc in next sc, *ch 1, sk next sc, dc in next sc; rep from * across, turn.

Row 3: Ch 1, sc in first ch-1 sp, *ch 5, sk next ch-1 sp, sc in next ch-1 sp; rep from * across, turn.

Row 4: Ch 1, *7 sc in next ch-5 sp; rep from * across, turn.

Row 5: Ch 5, sk 3 sc, sc in next sc, *ch 5, sk next 6 sc, sc in next sc; rep from * to last 3 sc, ch 3, dc in last sc, turn.

Row 6: Ch 1, sc in ch-3 sp, *ch 5, sc in next ch-5 sp; rep from * across. Fasten off.

BODY TRIM

With smaller hook and RS facing, join yarn with sl st to bottom corner of left front.

Row 1: Ch 1 (counts as first sc), sc 45 (47, 49, 51, 52) across left front to seam; sc 87 (91, 95, 99, 105) across back to seam; sc 45 (47, 49, 51, 52) across right front—177 (185, 193, 201, 209) sts, turn.

Rows 2–6: Work as for sleeve trim. Fasten off.

BUTTONBANDS AND NECK TRIM

Place markers for buttonholes on right front, the first at the beg of trim, the last at the top neck corners, space rem 5 evenly bet. With smaller hook and RS facing, attach yarn to bottom corner of right-front trim. Ch 1 (counts as first sc), sc up right front to corner, 3 sc in corner st, sc around neck edge to left-front corner, 3 sc in corner st, sc down left front, turn.

Next row: Work 4 rep of Picot Edge (see Stitch Guide), sc up left front to 3 corner sts, Picot Edge around neck sts to 3 right-front corner sts, turn.

Buttonhole

Ch 4, skip next 2 sc, work Picot Edge st to next m; rep buttonhole at each marker, ending with Picot Edge st to end. Fasten off. Sew sleeve seams; sew sleeves into armholes. Weave in loose ends and wet-block. 🖋

KRISTEN TENDYKE is the author of *Finish-Free Knits* (Interweave, 2012).

Trellis Pullover

BY ELISSA SUGISHITA

This flowing sweater is crocheted from side to side, creating a vertical stripe pattern that's slimming and has excellent drape. With only basic shaping, this unusual construction creates a high-end look.

Finished Size

36 (39, 42, 45)" (91.5 [99, 106.5, 114.5] cm) bust circumference, loose fitting. Garment shown measures 39" (99 cm).

Yarn

Naturally Stella (100% bamboo; 191 yds [175 m]/1¾ oz [50 g]; (2)): #349 lavender, 9 (10, 11, 12) skeins. Yarn distributed by Fiber Trends.

Note: This yarn has been discontinued. Please substitute a fingering-weight (#1 – Super Fine) yarn that works up to the same gauge.

Hook Size

E/4 (3.5 mm). Adjust hook size if necessary to obtain the correct gauge.

Notions

Yarn needle.

Gauge

20 sts and 12 rows = 4" (10 cm) in dc patt.

Note

* This sweater is worked from side to side. Gauge is especially important for this garment because you cannot add to the length later.

Back

Ch 97 (99, 101, 103).

Row 1: Dc in 3rd ch from hook and each ch across, turn.

Rows 2–3: Ch 3 (counts as dc), dc in 2nd dc and in each dc across, turn—95 (97, 109, 111) dc.

Row 4: Ch 4 (counts as tr), *ch 1, sk next st, tr in next st; rep from * across, turn.

Rep Rows 1–4 until piece measures 18 (19½, 21, 22½)" (45.5 [49.5, 53.25, 57.25] cm) from beg. Fasten off.

Front

Work as for back until piece measures 4 (4½, 5, 5½)" (10.25 [11.5, 12.75, 14] cm).

SHAPE NECK

Dec 1 st at neck edge every row 8 times maintaining the patt. Work in patt for 4 (4½, 5, 5½)" (10.25 [11.5, 12.75, 14] cm). Inc 1 st at neck edge every row 8 times maintaining the patt.

Cont in patt for 4 (4½, 5, 5½)" (10.25 [11.5, 12.75, 14] cm) until piece measures 18 (19½, 21, 22½)" (45.5 [49.5, 53.25, 57.25] cm) from beg. Fasten off.

Sleeves

Ch 79 (81, 83, 85).

Row 1: Dc in 3rd ch from hook and each ch across, turn—77 (79, 81, 83) dc.

Rows 2–3: Ch 3 (counts as dc), dc in 2nd dc and in each dc across, turn.

Row 4: Ch 4 (counts as tr), *ch 1, sk next st, tr in next st; rep from * across, turn.

Rep Rows 1–4 until piece measures 14 (14, 15½, 15½)" (35.5 [35.5, 39.5, 39.5] cm), ending with Row 3. Fasten off.

BEGIN WRIST CUFFS

With RS facing, join yarn with sl st to one short edge of sleeve, work 45 (45, 50, 50) sc evenly across, turn. Work 3 rows dc, then 1 row sc, then 1 row rev sc (see Glossary). Fasten off.

Waistband

Ch 25.

Row 1: Dc in 3rd ch from hook and each ch across, turn.

Row 2: Ch 3 (counts as dc), dc in 2nd dc and in each dc across, turn.

Rep Row 2 until sash measures 90" (228.5 cm) or desired length. Fasten off.

Finishing

Block each piece according to the yarn label. Using yarn needle, sew shoulder seams. Sew in sleeves aligning the center to shoulder seams. Sew the underarm and side seams.

NECKLINE

Join yarn with sl st to neck at right shoulder seam, work 48 (50, 52, 54) sc along back neck and 54 (56, 58, 60) sc along front neck.

Next rnd: Work rev sc around, sl st in first st to join. Fasten off.

Sew sash to waistline aligning center of sash to right side seam. Weave in loose ends. 🖋

ELISSA SUGISHITA is an avid crocheter and knitter with a background in the children's clothing industry and a love for clothing design. She currently works as a computer technician for a major New York publishing company.

ZZ Topper
BY DORIS CHAN

The zigzag stitch pattern of this relaxed pullover makes six "spokes" that give the piece a trapeze shape and a flattering line. Essentially a round poncho closed at the sides for armholes, this simple top is flexible and versatile.

Finished Size

50 (56, 60)" (127 [142, 152.5] cm) bust circumference. Garment shown measures 50" (127 cm). Garment is designed to be loose; choose a size 10" (25.5 cm) greater than your bust circumference.

Yarn

South West Trading Company A-Maizing (100% corn fiber; 142 yd [130 m]/1¾ oz [50 g]): #369 black, 5 (6, 7) balls.

Note: This yarn has been discontinued. Please substitute a sportweight (#2 – Fine) yarn that works up to the same gauge.

Hook Size

J/10 (6 mm). Adjust hook size if necessary to obtain the correct gauge.

Notions

Yarn needle.

Gauge

8 sts and 5 rows = 4" (10 cm) in tr.

Stitch Guide

Shell (sh): 5 tr in same st.

Notes

* The zigzagging strips are created with rows of offset shells alternating with increasing mesh panels of treble crochet. The two treble crochets at each edge of the mesh panels are worked in the top loops of the next stitch, but the treble stitch(es) in the middle of the panel are made in the space between stitches as follows: Yarn over two times, insert hook into the space between the stitches, make treble crochet.

* Top is made from the neck down in joined rounds that are worked back and forth. Increases are made every round in each mesh panel.

Top

Fsc (see page 38) 60 (66, 66), sl st in beg fsc to form a ring, being careful not to twist sts. Set up patt as foll:

SIZES 50 (56)" ONLY

Rnd 1: Ch 4, sk first fsc, tr in each of next 3 (4) fsc, *sk next 2 fsc, sh (see Stitch Guide) in next fsc, ch 2, sk next 2 fsc**, tr in each of next 5 (6) fsc*; rep from * to * 4 times; rep from * to ** once, tr in last fsc, sl st in top of turning chain (tch), turn—5 (6) tr in each of six mesh panels.

SIZE 60" ONLY

Rnd 1: Ch 4, sk first fsc, *tr in each of next 4 fsc, 2 tr in next fsc, sk next 2, sh in next fsc, ch 2, sk next 2 fsc, 2 tr in next fsc*; rep from * to * 5 times omitting last 2 tr, tr in same fsc as beg, sl st in top of tch, turn—8 tr in each of six mesh panels.

ALL SIZES

Inc 1 tr in each panel every row as foll:

Rnd 2: Ch 4 (counts as next-to-last tr of beg panel), tr in next tr, *sk next ch-2 sp, sh in first tr of next sh, ch 2, sk rem 4 tr of sh, tr in each of next 2 tr of panel, tr in next 2 (3, 5) sps between tr, tr in each of last 2 tr of panel; rep from * 5 times omitting last 2 tr, sl st in top of tch, turn—6 (7, 9) tr in each of six mesh panels.

Rnd 3: Ch 4 (counts as 2nd tr of beg panel), *tr in each sp between tr to last 2 tr of panel, tr in each of last 2 tr of panel, sk next ch-2 sp, sh in first tr of next sh, ch 2, sk rem 4 tr of sh, tr in each of next 2 tr of panel; rep from * 5 times omitting last tr, sl st in top of tch, turn—7 (8, 10) tr in each of six mesh panels.

Rnd 4: Ch 4 (counts as next-to-last tr of beg panel), tr in next tr, *sk next ch-2 sp, sh in first tr of next sh, ch 2, sk rem 4 tr of sh, tr in each of next 2 tr of panel, tr in each sp between tr to last 2 tr of panel, tr in each of last 2 tr of panel; rep from * 5 times omitting last 2 tr, sl st in top of tch; turn—8 (9, 11) tr in each of six mesh panels.

SIZE 50" ONLY

Rnds 5–15: Rep Rnds 3–4 five times, then Rnd 3 once more—19 tr in each of 6 mesh panels.

SIZES 56 (60)" ONLY

Rnds 5–17: Rep Rnds 3–4 six times, then Rnd 3 once more—22 (24) tr in each of six mesh panels.

Join front and back at underarms leaving armholes unworked as foll: Joining rnd: Ch 4 (counts as next-to-last tr of beg panel), tr in next tr, *sk next ch-2 sp, sh in first tr of next sh, ch 2, sk rem 4 tr of sh, tr in each of next 2 tr of panel, tr in each sp between tr to last 2 tr of panel, tr in each of last 2 tr of panel*, **sk next ch-2 sp, sh in first tr of next sh, ch 2, sk rem 4 tr of sh, tr in each of next 2 tr of panel, tr in each of next 8 (9, 10) sps between tr, sk rem tr of same panel, sk next sh, sk first 10 (11, 12) tr of next panel, tr in each of next 8 (10, 11) sps between tr to last 2 tr of panel, tr in each of last 2 tr of panel**; rep from * to * once, rep from ** to ** once, omitting last 2 tr, sl st in top of tch, turn—20 (23, 25) tr in each of four mesh panels of body.

Body

Work in patt, cont to inc each panel as foll: Rep Rnds 3 and 4 of top 3 (4, 4) times—26 (31, 33) tr in each of 4 mesh panels in last rnd. Fasten off. Top should have 22 (26, 26) rnds total. Shape neck edge: There is no obvious RS or WS. Choose which side you want to be RS. With RS facing, join yarn with sl st in any fsc of neck, ch 1, sc in same st, sc in each st around, sl st

Finishing

Weave in loose ends. Block according to instructions on yarn label. 🌿

DORIS CHAN is the author of *Amazing Crochet Lace* (2006), *Everyday Crochet* (2007), and *Convertible Crochet* (2013), all from Potter Craft.

Stitch Pattern

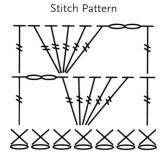

Key

⬭   chain (ch)

╳   single crochet (sc)

╪   treble crochet (tr)

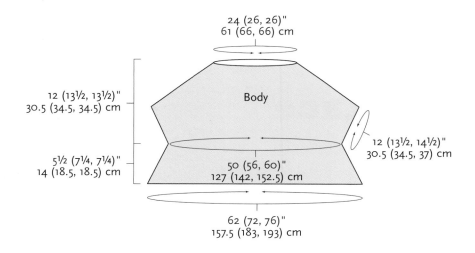

24 (26, 26)"
61 (66, 66) cm

Body

12 (13½, 13½)"
30.5 (34.5, 34.5) cm

12 (13½, 14½)"
30.5 (34.5, 37) cm

5½ (7¼, 7¼)"
14 (18.5, 18.5) cm

50 (56, 60)"
127 (142, 152.5) cm

62 (72, 76)"
157.5 (183, 193) cm

Linen and Lace Cardigan

BY KATHY MERRICK

Horizontal ribs paired with lighter, open lace-work create the flattering texture of this jacket. Sewn seams on one side and picot edging on the other help to keep the ribbed centers from growing too much in length during wear. The four-row lace pattern is easily memorized and progresses quickly.

Center-Back Panel

Ch 56 (66, 61, 71).

Row 1: Hdc in 3rd ch from hook and in each ch across, turn.

Row 2: Ch 2 (counts as hdc), sk first hdc, hdc through back lp only (blo) of each hdc to end of row, turn.

Rep Row 2 until piece measures 27¼ (28¼, 29¼, 30¼)" from beg. Ch 2, hdc blo in each of the next 8 (10, 12, 14) sts, hdc2tog blo (see Stitch Guide), hdc blo in next hdc, turn. Work 1 row even. Fasten off. With WS facing, join yarn with sl st 11 (13, 15, 17) sts from opposite edge of piece. Ch 2, hdc blo in next st, hdc2tog blo, hdc blo in each of the next 9 (11, 13, 15) sts, turn. Work 1 row even. Fasten off.

Center-Front Panels
(make 2)

Ch 29 (34, 32, 37). Work as for center-back panel until piece measures 24½ (25½, 26½, 27½)".

SHAPE NECK

Row 1: Work even in hdc blo across row until 7 (9, 11, 13) sts rem, turn.

Row 2: Ch 2, hdc blo in next st, hdc2tog blo, hdc blo in each st across—1 st dec'd.

Dec 1 st at neck edge every row until 10 (12, 14, 16) sts rem. Work even to match back panel length. Fasten off.

Lace Panels
(make 2)

SLEEVE

Ch 40 (44, 48, 52). Work 4 rows of lace patt (see Stitch Guide) over 37 (41, 45, 49) sts, then inc 1 st by working 2 dc in last sc of previous row at each end on every Row 4. At the same time, inc 1 rep every Row 2 by working (sc, ch 3, dc in sc just made) in last ch-5 sp. Cont in lace patt for a total of 11 (11, 12, 12) patt reps. Work Rows 1 and 2 again. Fasten off.

ADD SIDE PANELS

Ch 93 (97, 100, 104). With RS facing, join ch with sl st to left side of sleeve. Work Row 3 of lace patt across sleeve, ch 96 (100, 103, 107), turn—280 (292, 308, 320)

Finished Size

36 (40, 44, 48)" (91.5 [101.5, 112, 122] cm) bust circumference, with fronts meeting. Jacket shown measures 40" (101.5).

Yarn

Louet Euroflax Sportweight (100% linen; 270 yd [240 m]/3½ oz [100 g]): grape, 6 (7, 7, 8) skeins.

Hook Size

F/5 (3.75 mm). Adjust hook size if necessary to obtain the correct gauge.

Notions

Yarn needle.

Gauge

20 sts and 12 rows = 4" (10 cm) in hdc rib. *Note: Rib can be difficult to measure—measure gauge with piece lying on flat surface without stretching.*

20 dc = 4" (10 cm) in lace patt; one 4-row rep of lace patt = 1½" (3.8 cm).

Stitch Guide

Hdc2tog blo Decrease: Yo, insert hook in back lp only of next st and draw up a lp, yo, insert hook in back lp only of next st and draw up a lp (5 lps on hook), yo, draw through all lps on hook—1 st dec'd.

Lace Pattern (multiple of 4 sts +1)
Set-up row: Dc in 4th ch from hook (counts as dc), dc in each ch to end, turn.

Row 1: Ch 1, sc in first st, *ch 5, sk 3 sts, sc in next st; rep from * to end, turn.

Row 2: Ch 5 (counts as dc, ch 2), *sc in next ch-5 sp, (ch 3, dc in sc just made); rep from *, ending with sc in last ch-5 sp, ch 2, dc in last sc, turn.

Row 3: Ch 1, sc in first dc, *ch 3, sc in next ch-3 sp; rep from *, ending with sc in 3rd ch of tch, turn.

Row 4: Ch 3 (counts as dc), *3 dc in ch-3 sp, dc in next sc; rep from * to end, turn.

Note

* Garment is worked in pieces: one ribbed center back, two ribbed center fronts, and two identical lace pieces that each make up one sleeve and side panel. Pieces are sewn together, creating garment as shown in schematic.

---

sts. Dc in 4th ch from hook (counts as dc), dc in each st to end, turn. Work 2 (2, 3, 3) reps of lace patt. Fasten off.

Finishing

Steam lace panels to smooth and flatten. Sew center-back panel to center-front panels at shoulders, reversing one front to mirror the other. Sew lace panels to center panels, stretching lace slightly to fit. Sew sleeve and side seams. With RS facing, join yarn with sl st at lower left back, sc in each st across back, up right front, around neck, down left front and back to beg, working 3 hdc in all corner sts; sl st to first sc to join. Do not turn.

Next rnd: 2 sc in first st, *(sc, ch 4, sc) in next sc, sc in each of next 3 sts; rep from * until 2 sts before neck shaping.

MAKE TIE

Sc in next sc, ch 101 (101, 106, 106), turn. Sl st in each ch back to neck, sc in same sc. Cont in patt until 2 sts after neck shaping on opposite side. Make second tie as for first. Cont in patt to end of rnd. Fasten off.

Weave in all loose ends. Press edging if necessary.

KATHY MERRICK of New Hope, Pennsylvania, taught herself to crochet after her beloved grandmother refused to deal with her extreme left-handedness.

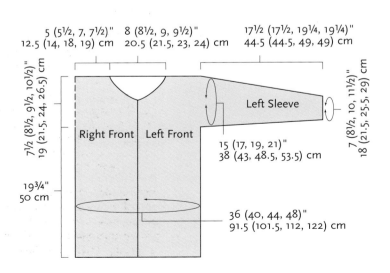

5 (5½, 7, 7½)"
12.5 (14, 18, 19) cm

8 (8½, 9, 9½)"
20.5 (21.5, 23, 24) cm

17½ (17½, 19¼, 19¼)"
44.5 (44.5, 49, 49) cm

7½ (8½, 9½, 10½)"
19 (21.5, 24, 26.5) cm

7 (8½, 10, 11½)"
18 (21.5, 25.5, 29) cm

Right Front   Left Front

Left Sleeve

15 (17, 19, 21)"
38 (43, 48.5, 53.5) cm

19¾"
50 cm

36 (40, 44, 48)"
91.5 (101.5, 112, 122) cm

Sera Lace Top

BY DORIS CHAN

This pullover is roomy and stretchy, with a wide neckline; long, flared sleeves; and picot trim. Flaring gently to mid-hip, it's perfect for an evening of elegance or a day of feeling pretty.

Upper Body

Fsc (see Glossary) 72 (72, 72, 80, 80, 80), sl st in beg fsc to form ring, being careful not to twist sts. Set up 12 (12, 12, 14, 14, 16) reps with incs as foll. Sizes 48 (52, 56)" 122 [132, 142] cm) have "cheat" sts at center-front and -back neck.)

SIZES 36 (40, 44)" ONLY

Rnd 1: (RS) Ch 3, 4 dc in same fsc, *[sk next fsc, sc in next fsc, ch 5, sk next fsc, sc in next fsc, sk next fsc, sh in next fsc]** 4 times, (ch 2, sh) in same fsc for corner, rep from * to ** 2 times*, (ch 2, sh) in same fsc for corner; rep from * to *, placing last sh in same fsc as beg, ch 1, sc in top of beg ch, turn—16 sh.

SIZES 48 (52)" ONLY

Rnd 1: (RS) Ch 3, 4 dc in same fsc, *[sk next fsc, sc in next fsc, ch 5, sk next fsc, sc in next fsc, sk next fsc, sh in next fsc]** 2 times, sc in next fsc, ch 5, sk next fsc, sc in next fsc, sh in next fsc; rep from * to ** 2 times, (ch 2, sh) in same fsc for corner; rep from * to ** 2 times*, (ch 2, sh) in same fsc for corner; rep from * to *, placing last sh in same fsc as beg, ch 1, sc in top of beg ch, turn—18 sh.

SIZE 56" ONLY

Rnd 1: (RS) Ch 3, 4 dc in same fsc, *sk next fsc, sc in next fsc, ch 5, sk next fsc, sc in next fsc, sk next fsc, sh in next fsc**, [sc in next fsc, ch 5, sk next fsc, sc in next fsc, sh in next fsc] 4 times, rep from * to **, (ch 2, sh) in same fsc for corner, rep from * to ** 2 times*, (ch 2, sh) in same fsc for corner; rep from * to *, placing last sh in same fsc as beg, ch 1, sc in top of beg ch, turn—20 sh.

Place corner marker at each ch-2 sp. Move m up each rnd.

ALL SIZES

Rnd 2: (WS) Ch 1, sc in first ch-sp, ch 5, sc in 3rd dc of next sh, *[ch 5, sc in next ch-5 sp, ch 5, sc in 3rd dc of next sh]**; rep from * to ** to next corner ch-2 sp, ch 5, sc in corner ch-2 sp, ch 5, sc in 3rd dc of next sh*; rep from * to * 2 times; rep from * to ** to end, ch 5, sl st in beg sc, turn.

Rnd 3 (inc rnd): Ch 3, 4 dc in first sc, *[sc in next ch-5 sp, ch 5, sk next sc, sc in next ch-5 sp, sh in next sc] to next corner, placing last sh in next corner sc**, (ch 2, sh) in same corner sc*; rep from * to * 2 times; rep from * to ** once, place last sh

Finished Size

36 (40, 44, 48, 52, 56)" (91.5 [101.5, 112, 122, 132, 142] cm) bust circumference. Sweater shown measures 36" (91.5 cm).

Yarn

Filatura Di Crosa Sera (84% wool, 11% viscose, 5% polyamide; 147 yd [135 m]/1¾ oz [50 g]; (**2**)): #40 silver grey, 5 (6, 6, 7, 7, 8) balls. Yarn distributed by Tahki Stacy Charles.

Note: This yarn has been discontinued. Please substitute a DK weight (#3 – Light) yarn that works up to the same gauge.

Hook Size

G/7 (4.5 mm). Adjust hook size if necessary to obtain the correct gauge.

Notions

Removable stitch markers (m).

Gauge

13 fsc = 4" (10 cm); (shell, sc, ch 5, sc) 2 times in patt and 8 rows = 4" (10 cm).

Stitch Guide

Shell (sh): 5 dc in same st or sp.

Picot-sh: (3 dc, ch 3, sl st in top of dc just made, 2 dc) in same st.

Shell Trellis Patt (worked in joined rnds)

Rnd 1: (WS) Ch 1, sc in first ch-sp, *ch 5, sc in 3rd dc of next sh, ch 5, sc in next ch-5 sp; rep from * around, omitting last sc, and ending with sl st in first sc, turn.

Rnd 2: (RS) Ch 3, 2 dc in same sc, *sc in next ch-5 sp, ch 5, sk next sc, sc in next ch-5 sp, sh in next sc; rep from * around, omitting last sh on final rep, and ending with 2 dc in same sc as beg, sl st in top of beg ch, turn.

Rnd 3: Ch 1, sc in same dc, ch 5, sc in next ch-5 sp, *ch 5, sc in 3rd dc of next sh, ch 5, sc in next ch-5 sp; rep from * around, ending with ch 2, dc in first sc, turn.

Rnd 4: Ch 1, sc in first ch-sp, sh in next sc, sc in next ch-5 sp, *ch 5, sk next sc, sc in next ch-5 sp, sh in next sc, sc in next ch-5 sp; rep from * around, ending with ch 2, sk next sc, dc in first sc, turn.

Rep Rows 3–4 for patt.

Notes

* This fabric grows when worn, particularly the sleeves. Keep this in mind before deciding to lengthen.

* Top is made from the neck down in joined rounds worked back and forth. Incs in patt are made at each of four "corners" and shape the raglan-style shoulders of the yoke. Mark the ch-sp or st at each corner and move markers (m) up as you go.

---

in same corner sc as beg, ch 1, sc in top of beg ch, turn—20 (20, 20, 22, 22, 24) sh.

SIZE 36" ONLY

Rnds 4–8: Rep Rnds 2–3 two times, then Rnd 2 once more—28 sh.

SIZE 40" ONLY

Rnds 4–10: Rep Rnds 2–3 three times, then Rnd 2 once more—32 sh.

SIZES 44 (48)" ONLY

Rnds 4–12: Rep Rnds 2–3 four times, then Rnd 2 once more—36 (38) sh.

SIZES 52 (56)" ONLY

Rnds 4–14: Rep Rnds 2–3 five times, then Rnd 2 once more— 42 (44) sh.

ALL SIZES

Work Rnds 2–4 of est patt once more. Moving toward armhole, join front and back at underarms as foll: Joining Rnd: (WS) Ch 1, sc in first ch-sp, *ch 1, fsc 7 for underarm, sk 6 (7, 8, 8, 9, 9) sh of armhole, sc in next corner ch-5 sp, [ch 5, sc in 3rd dc of next sh, ch 5, sc in next ch-5 sp] across*, placing last sc in next corner ch-5 sp; rep from * to *, omitting last sc on final rep, sl st in beg sc.

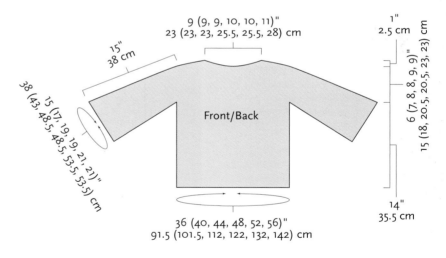

9 (9, 9, 10, 10, 11)"
23 (23, 23, 25.5, 25.5, 28) cm

15"
38 cm

15 (17, 19, 19, 21, 21)"
38 (43, 48.5, 48.5, 53.5, 53.5) cm

Front/Back

1"
2.5 cm

6 (7, 8, 8, 9, 9)"
15 (18, 20.5, 20.5, 23, 23) cm

14"
35.5 cm

36 (40, 44, 48, 52, 56)"
91.5 (101.5, 112, 122, 132, 142) cm

Lower Body

Fill in patt over underarms, work even on 18 (20, 22, 24, 26, 28) sh as foll:

Rnd 1: (RS) Ch 3, 2 dc in same sc, *[sc in next ch-5 sp, ch 5, sk next sc, sc in next ch-5 sp, sh in next sc] to next underarm, placing sh in sc before fsc at underarm, sk next fsc, sc in next fsc, ch 5, sk next 3 fsc, sc in next fsc, sk rem fsc, sh in next sc; rep from *, omitting last sh, 2 dc in same sc as beg, sl st in top of beg ch, turn—18 (20, 22, 24, 26, 28) sh.

Rnds 2–24: [Work sh trellis patt (see Stitch Guide) Rnds 3–4, then Patt Rnds 1–4] 5 times, then work Rnd 1 once more.

Note: For shorter top, omit 2 rnds (1" [2.5 cm]) or work to desired length, end by working sh trellis patt Rnd 1 or 3. For longer top, add 2 rnds (1" [2.5 cm]) or work to desired length, end by working patt Rnd 1 or 3.

BEG LOWER-EDGE TRIM

(RS) Work same as sh trellis patt Rnd 2 except replace each sh with a picot-sh (see Stitch Guide), end with 2 dc in same sc as beg, sl st in top of beg ch, ch 3, sl st in top of same beg ch. Fasten off. If you altered the length and ended by working a Patt Rnd 3, then work trim same as patt Rnd 4, substituting picot sh for each sh, end with ch 5, sl st in beg sc. Fasten off.

Sleeves

With WS facing, join yarn with sl st in 4th base ch of fsc at center of underarm.

Rnd 1: Ch 1, sc in same base ch, ch 5, sk rem 3 base ch, sc in next corner ch-5 sp (same as joined at underarm), [ch 5, sc in 2nd dc of next sh, ch 5, sc in next ch-5 sp] 6 (7, 8, 8, 9, 9) times, placing sc in next corner ch-5 sp at join, ch 2, dc in beg sc, turn.

Rnds 2–27: Work sh trellis patt Rnd 4, then patt Rnds 1–4 six times, then patt Rnd 1 once more.

Next Rnd: Work picot trim around, sl st in beg sc. Fasten off.

Finishing

If your neck base ch has stretched, or if you prefer a slightly closer neckline, crochet the edging more firmly. Otherwise, work to gauge. With RS facing, join yarn with sl st in any fsc of neck, ch 1, sc in same fsc, sc in each fsc around, sl st in beg sc—72 (72, 72, 80, 80, 80) sc. Fasten off. Weave in loose ends; block to measurements. 🖋

- -

DORIS CHAN is the author of *Amazing Crochet Lace* (2006), *Everyday Crochet* (2007), and *Convertible Crochet* (2013), all from Potter Craft.

Key

○ Chain (ch)

● Slip st (sl st)

✕ Single crochet (sc)

⊤ Double crochet (dc)

⋀ 5-dc shell

⬡ Ch-3 picot

Picot-Shell Trim

Lower-Body Shell Trellis

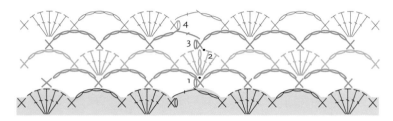

Marilyn Twin Set

BY SARAH BARBOUR

Channel 1950s stars of the silver screen in this retro twin set. A wispy mohair cardigan is paired with a fitted bra-style camisole for a set that travels from the office to an evening out.

Finished Size

Cardigan: 34 (37½, 41, 44¼, 47¾)" (86.5 [95, 104, 112.5, 121.5] cm) bust circumference; camisole: 30 (31¼, 34, 38¼, 41)" (76 [79.5, 86.5, 97, 104] cm) underbust. Set shown: cardigan measures 34" (86.5 cm), modeled with 2" (5 cm) negative ease.

Yarn

Blue Moon Fiber Arts Silkmo (70% kid mohair, 20% mulberry silk, 10% nylon; 794 yd [726 m]/3¾ oz [106 g]; (1)): rosebud (A); 1 skein.

Blue Moon Fiber Arts Geisha (70% kid mohair, 20% mulberry silk, 10% nylon; 995 yd [910 m]/8 oz [226 g]; (1)): rosebud (B), 1 skein.

Hook

Size F/5 (3.75 mm). Adjust hook size if necessary to obtain correct gauge.

Notions

Stitch markers (m); yarn needle; hooks and eyes; 2½–3½ yd (2.25-3.25 m) grosgrain ribbon for lining straps and band; sewing needle and matching thread.

Gauge

Cardigan: 20½ sts and 8 rows = 4" (10 cm) in iris patt. Camisole: 24 sts and 32 rows = 4" (10 cm) in sc and 20½ sts and 10 rows = 4" (10 cm) in iris patt.

Notes

* Cardigan is worked from the top down, working fronts and back at the same time.

* Cardigan sleeves are picked up and worked down from body in the round, joining at the end of each row and turning.

* Camisole begins with the band. Body is worked first in rows, then in the round, joining at the end of each row and turning. Left-front and right-front bodice are worked separately and then joined to band.

* To determine camisole band fit, measure around torso, just under bust, and choose the size closest to this measurement.

Stitch Guide

Iris patt (multiple of 4 sts +1)
Row 1: Ch 3, sk next ch, *(2 dc, ch 1, 2 dc) in next ch, sk next 3 ch; rep from * to last 2 ch, sk next ch, dc in next ch, turn.

Row 2: Ch 3, sk first 3 dc, *(2 dc, ch 1, 2 dc) in next ch-1 sp, sk next 4 dc; rep from * to last ch-1 sp, (2 dc, ch 1, 2 dc) in ch-1 sp, sk last 2 dc, dc in top of tch, turn.

Rep Row 2 for patt.

Inc row: Work in patt to marker (m), work ([2 dc, ch 1] 3 times, 2 dc) in each marked ch-1 sp, move m up to center of 3 ch-1 sps.

38, 40.5] cm) from armholes. Fasten off. Join B, sc in each st and ch-1 sp across. Fasten off.

LEFT SLEEVE

Rnd 1: With WS facing, join A at 2nd m, ch 3, (2 dc, ch 1, 2 dc) in same ch-sp, cont in iris patt around working (2 dc, ch 1, 2 dc) in last sp before beg ch-3, sl st in beg ch-3 to join, turn—15 (17, 19, 19, 21) ch-1 sps.

Rnds 2–5 (5, 6, 7, 8): Work even in iris patt. Fasten off.

RIGHT SLEEVE

Rnd 1: With WS facing, join A at first m, ch 3, (2 dc, ch 1, 2 dc) in same sp, cont work in iris patt around working (2 dc, ch 1, 2 dc) in last sp.

Rep Rnds 2–5 (5, 6, 7, 8) of left sleeve.

Finishing

With RS facing, join B to left-front neck edge, sc down left front to hem. Fasten off. With RS facing, join B to right-front lower edge, sc up right front to neckline. Fasten off.

TIES

Join B at left edge about 7" (18 cm) down from neck edge, ch 37, turn, sk first ch, sc in rem ch across. Fasten off. Rep for right edge.

Camisole

BAND

Ch 181 (189, 205, 229, 245).

Row 1: Sc in 2nd ch from hook and each ch across, turn—180 (188, 204, 228, 244) sc.

Place marker (pm) in 46th and 135th (48th and 141st, 52nd and 153rd, 58th and 171st, and 62nd and 183rd) sc for bodice placement.

Rows 2–8: Ch 1, sc across, turn.

Row 9: Sl st in first 4 sc, work Row 1 of iris patt (see Stitch Guide) to last 4 sc, turn leaving rem sts unworked.

Work 5 (5, 6, 6, 7) rows even in iris patt.

Next row: Work iris patt across, sl st in 3rd ch of beg ch-3 to join in the rnd. Rep last row until work measures 9 (9, 9½, 10, 11)" (22.75 [22.75, 24.25, 25.5, 28] cm) from band. Fasten off and set aside.

Cardigan

With B, ch 105 (105, 105, 121, 121).

Foundation row: Sc in 2nd ch from hook and each ch across—104 (104, 104, 120, 120) sts. Fasten off B.

Rnd 1: Join A, work Row 1 of iris patt (see Stitch Guide).

SIZES 34 (37½, 41¼)" ONLY

Place marker (pm) in 5th, 9th, 18th, and 22nd ch-1 sps.

SIZES 44¼ (47¾)" ONLY

Place marker (pm) in 6th, 10th, 21st, and 25th ch-1 sps.

ALL SIZES

Row 2: Work inc row (see Stitch Guide).

Rows 3–4: Work Row 2 of iris patt.

Rep Rows 2–4 five (six, seven, seven, eight) times—66 (74, 82, 86, 94) ch-1 sps.

DIVIDE FOR SLEEVES

Row 1: Work iris patt in next 10 (11, 12, 13, 14) ch-1 sps, pm, sk next 13 (15, 17, 17, 19) ch-1 sps, work iris patt in next 20 (22, 24, 26, 28) ch-1 sps, pm, sk next 13 (15, 17, 17, 19) ch-1 sps, cont in iris patt to end—40 (44, 48, 52, 56) ch-1 sps.

Work even in iris patt until work measures 14 (14, 14½, 15, 16)" (35.5 [35.5, 36.75,

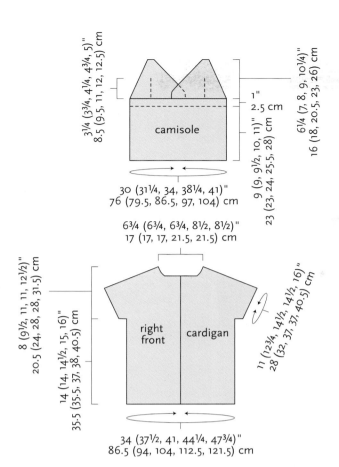

LEFT-FRONT BODICE

Ch 28 (32, 36, 40, 42).

Row 1: Sc in 2nd ch from hook and in each ch across, turn—27 (31, 35, 39, 41) sc.

Row 2: (RS) Ch 1, pm to mark RS of work, sc in each st to end.

Rows 3–25 (29, 33, 37, 41): Rep Row 2.

Row 26 (30, 34, 38, 42): Rep Row 2, turn work 90 degrees, work 24 (26, 30, 34, 38) sc in row-ends, turn—50 (56, 64, 72, 78) sts.

Rows 27–52 (31–60, 35–68, 39–76, 43–84): Ch 1, sc across, turn—50 (56, 64, 72, 78) sts.

Work short-rows as foll:

Next row: Ch 1, sc across, work 2 (4, 4, 4, 4) sc along edge, sl st in next st, turn, sc to end—52 (60, 68, 76, 82) sc.

Next row: Work to last sc, sl st in last sc of prev row, turn, sc to end. Rep last row 1 (1, 2, 2, 3) times.

Next row: Sc in next 36 (48, 56, 64, 70) sc, sl st in next st, turn, sc to end. Next row:

Sc to last 5 (5, 6, 6, 7) sts, sl st in next sc, turn, sc to end, turn. Rep last row 3 (3, 4, 4, 5) times.

Next row: (WS) Sc in next 43 (49, 56, 64, 73) sc, 3 sc in next sc, sc in next sc, pm in sc just made, sc in next 5 (5, 7, 7, 9) sc, 3 sc in last st of row, sc in every other row-end down armhole edge. Fasten off and set aside.

RIGHT-FRONT BODICE

Rep Rows 1–26 (30, 34, 38, 42) of left-front bodice. Fasten off.

Next row: Join B in bottom right corner in beg ch of right-front bodice, work 24 (26, 30, 34, 38) sc in row-ends, sc across top of bra—50 (56, 64, 72, 78) sts. Cont as for left-front bodice beg with Row 27 (31, 35, 39, 43).

Finishing
JOIN BODICE

With front of body facing you, sew right-front bodice to body band with RS facing and beg in left m. With front of body facing you, sew left-front bodice to body band

with RS facing, lining up last st to be sewn with right m and overlapping left-front bodice over right-front bodice. Sew left-front bodice to right-front at overlap.

STRAP

Row 1: (RS) Join in marked st, sc in next 7 (7, 9, 9, 11) sc, turn.

Row 2: Ch 1, sc across, turn—7 (7, 9, 9,11) sc.

Rep Row 2 to desired strap length. Fasten off and sew to band. Rep for right front. Weave in loose ends. Block to measurements. Sew grosgrain ribbon to backs of straps and band. Sew hooks and eyes onto edges of band. 🖋

- -

SARAH BARBOUR lives in Urbana, Illinois, where the weather is far from perfect–but is always just right for another crochet project. Visit her online at atropeknits.com.

Finished Size

36 (40, 44, 48, 52)" (91.5 [101.5, 112, 122, 132] cm) bust circumference, buttoned. Garment shown measures 36" (91.5 cm), modeled with 2" (5 cm) ease.

Yarn

KnitPicks Cotlin (70% tanguis cotton, 30% linen; 123 yd [112 m]/1¾ oz [50 g]; (**3**)): #24836 lilac (MC), 7 (8, 8, 9, 10) balls; #24835 cerise (CC1), #24467 blackberry (CC2) and #24462 sprout (CC3), 1 ball each.

Hook Sizes

E/4 (3.5 mm), G/6 (4 mm). Adjust hook size if necessary to obtain correct gauge.

Notions

Yarn needle; three 13 mm buttons.

Gauge

8 V-sts = 4" (10 cm) and 8 rows = 3" (7.5 cm) in V-st patt with larger hook.

Notes

* Larger hook is used for garment; smaller hook is used for flowers and leaves.

* In V-st patt, RS rows tend to make the fabric flare out. This tendency is controlled by WS rows. For accurate measurements, finish all pieces with a WS row.

* Thoroughly wet-block garment for ideal drape.

Arboretum Cardigan

BY ANNETTE PETAVY

This simple cardigan is spiced up with flower and leaf motifs scattered across the neckline and shoulder.

Stitch Guide

V-stitch (V-st): (Dc, ch 1, dc) in same st or sp.

V-st patt (worked over uneven number of sts)
Ch an even number.

Row 1: (WS) Sc in 2nd ch from hook, *ch 1, sk 1 ch, sc in next ch; rep from * across, turn.

Row 2: (RS) Ch 2 (does not count as dc), dc in first st, V-st (see above) in each sc to last sc, dc in last sc, turn.

Row 3: Ch 1, sc in first st, *ch 1, sc in ch-1 sp of next V-st; rep from * to last st, ch 1, sc in last st, turn.

Rep Rows 2–3 for patt.

Always finish piece with a WS row (see Notes).

Decreases and increases in middle of row

Decrease V-st (dec V-st), worked on RS row: After V-st just before dec, sk (ch and sc), V-st in next ch-sp, sk (sc and ch), V-st in next sc.

Increase V-st (inc V-st), worked on RS row: After V-st just before inc, V-st in next ch-sp, V-st after inc in next sc.

Decreases at edge of work

Slanted dec at beg of row (beg-dec): Ch 2 (does not count as dc), dc in next sc, V-st in next sc, cont in patt.

Slanted dec at end of row (end-dec): Work in patt until 2 sc (or indicated number of sts) rem, dc2tog (see Glossary) over next 2 sc, turn. On next row, treat dc2tog as first dc in row.

Back

With larger hook and MC, ch 76 (84, 92, 100, 108).

Work even in V-st patt (see Stitch Guide) until work measures 2¼ (2¼, 2¼, 2¼, 4)" (5.5 [5.5, 5.5, 5.5, 10] cm), ending with a WS row—36 (40, 44, 48, 52) V-sts on RS rows.

SHAPE WAIST

Dec row: (RS) Work 11 (12, 13, 15, 16) V-sts, dec V-st (see Stitch Guide), cont in patt until 13 (14, 15, 17, 18) V-sts rem, dec V-st, cont in patt to end of row, turn—34 (38, 42, 46, 50) V-sts.

Work 1 row even in patt.

Rep last 2 rows 2 times—30 (34, 38, 42, 46) V-sts.

Work even in patt until piece measures 6 (6¾, 6¾, 6¾, 7¾)" (15 [17, 17, 17, 19.5] cm) from beg, ending with a WS row.

SHAPE BUST

Inc row: (RS) Work 11 (12, 13, 15, 16) V-sts, inc V-st (see Stitch Guide), cont in patt until 11 (12, 13, 15, 16) V-sts rem, inc V-st, cont in patt to end of row, turn—32 (36, 40, 44, 48) V-sts.

Work 1 row even in patt.

Rep last 2 rows 2 times—36 (40, 44, 48, 52) V-sts.

Work even in patt until piece measures 12½ (13¼, 12½, 13½, 14)" (31.5 [33.5, 31.5, 34.5, 35.5] cm) from beg, ending with a WS row.

SHAPE ARMHOLES

Row 1: (RS) Sl st in first 5 (7, 9, 13, 15) sts, beg-dec (see Stitch Guide), cont in patt until 3 (4, 5, 7, 8) V-sts rem, end-dec (see Stitch Guide), turn leaving rem sts unworked—3 (4, 5, 7, 8) V-sts dec'd at each edge, 30 (32, 34, 34, 36) V-sts.

Row 2: (WS) Work even in patt.

Work slanted dec at beg and at end of RS rows 1 (2, 2, 1, 2) times—1 (1, 2, 1, 2) V-sts dec at each edge, 28 (30, 30, 32, 32) V-sts.

Work even in patt until piece measures 20 (20¾, 20¾, 21¾, 22¾)" (51 [52.5, 52.5, 55, 58] cm) from beg, ending with a WS row.

SHAPE SHOULDERS AND BACK NECK

Next row: (RS) Sl st in first 4 sts, sc in next 4 sts, hdc in next 4 (5, 4, 5, 5) sts, dc in next 4 (5, 4, 5, 5) sts, dc2tog (see Glossary) over next 2 sc. Fasten off.

Sk center 10 (10, 12, 12, 12) sc, join yarn with dc2tog over next 2 sc, dc in next 4 (5, 4, 5, 5) sts, hdc in next 4 (5, 4, 5, 5) sts, sc in next 4 sts, leave rem 4 sts unworked. Fasten off.

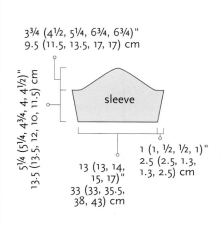

3¾ (4½, 5¼, 6¾, 6¾)"
9.5 (11.5, 13.5, 17, 17) cm

sleeve

5¼ (5¼, 4¾, 4, 4½)"
13.5 (13.5, 12, 10, 11.5) cm

13 (13, 14, 15, 17)"
33 (33, 35.5, 38, 43) cm

1 (1, ½, ½, 1)"
2.5 (2.5, 1.3, 1.3, 2.5) cm

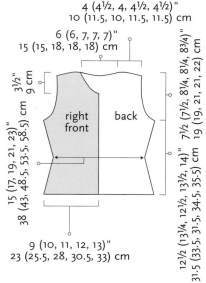

4 (4½, 4, 4½, 4½)"
10 (11.5, 10, 11.5, 11.5) cm

6 (6, 7, 7, 7)"
15 (15, 18, 18, 18) cm

3½"
9 cm

right front

back

15 (17, 19, 21, 23)"
38 (43, 48.5, 53.5, 58.5) cm

7½ (7½, 8¼, 8¼, 8¾)"
19 (19, 21, 21, 22) cm

12½ (13¼, 12½, 13½, 14)"
31.5 (33.5, 31.5, 34.5, 35.5) cm

9 (10, 11, 12, 13)"
23 (25.5, 28, 30.5, 33) cm

Left Front

With larger hook and MC, ch 40 (44, 48, 52, 56).

Work even in V-st patt until piece measures 2¼ (2¼, 2¼, 2¼, 4)" (5.5 [5.5, 5.5, 5.5, 10] cm), ending with a WS row—18 (20, 22, 24, 26) V-sts on RS rows.

SHAPE WAIST

Dec row: (RS) Work 11 (12, 13, 15, 16) V-sts, dec V-st, work in patt to end of row, turn—17 (19, 21, 23, 25) V-sts.

Work 1 row even in patt.

Rep last 2 rows 2 times—15 (17, 19, 21, 23) V-sts.

Work even in patt until piece measures 6 (6¾, 6¾, 6¾, 7¾)" (15 [17, 17, 17, 19.5] cm) from beg, ending with a WS row.

SHAPE BUST

Inc row: (RS) Work 11 (12, 13, 15, 16) V-sts, inc V-st, cont in patt to end of row, turn—16 (18, 20, 22, 24) V-sts.

Work 1 row even in patt.

Rep last 2 rows 2 times—18 (20, 22, 24, 26) V-sts.

Work even in patt until piece measures 12½ (13¼, 12½, 13½, 14)" (31.5, 33.5, 31.5, 34.5, 35.5] cm), ending with a WS row.

SHAPE ARMHOLE

Row 1: (RS) Sl st in first 5 (7, 9, 13, 15) sts, beg-dec, cont in patt to end, turn—3 (4, 5, 7, 8) V-sts dec'd at side seam, 15 (16, 17, 17, 18) V-sts.

Row 2: (WS) Work even in patt.

Work slanted dec at beg of row on RS row 1 (1, 2, 1, 2) times—1 (1, 2, 1, 2) V-sts dec'd at side edge, 14 (15, 15, 16, 16) V-sts.

Work even in patt until piece measures 17 (17¾, 17¾, 18¾, 19¾)" (43 [45, 45, 47.5, 50] cm), ending with a WS row.

SHAPE FRONT NECK

Row 1: (RS) Work in patt until 5 (5, 6, 6, 6) V-sts rem, end-dec, turn leaving rem sts unworked—5 (5, 6, 6, 6) V-sts dec'd at front edge, 9 (10, 9, 10, 10) V-sts.

Row 2: (WS) Work even in patt.

Work end-dec at end of row on RS row 2 times—7 (8, 7, 8, 8) V-sts.

Work even in patt until piece measures 20 (20¾, 20¾, 21¾, 22¾)" (51 [52.5, 52.5, 55, 58] cm), ending with a WS row.

SHAPE SHOULDER

Next row: (RS) Sl st in first 4 sts, sc in next 4 sts, hdc in next 4 (5, 4, 5, 5) sts, dc in next 5 (6, 5, 6, 6) sts. Fasten off.

Right Front

With larger hook and MC, ch 40 (44, 48, 52, 56).

Work even in V-st patt until piece measures 2¼ (2¼, 2¼, 2¼, 4)" (5.5 [5.5, 5.5, 5.5, 10] cm), ending with a WS row—18 (20, 22, 24, 26) V-sts on RS rows.

SHAPE WAIST

Dec row: (RS) Work in patt until 13 (14, 15, 17, 18) V-sts rem, dec V-st, cont in patt to end of row, turn—17 (19, 21, 23, 25) V-sts.

Work 1 row even in patt.

Rep last 2 rows 2 times—15 (17, 19, 21, 23) V-sts.

Work even in patt until piece measures 6 (6¾, 6¾, 6¾, 7¾)" (15 [17, 17, 17, 19.5] cm), ending with a WS row.

SHAPE BUST

Inc row: (RS) Work in patt until 11 (12, 13, 15, 16) V-sts rem, inc V-st, cont in patt to end of row, turn—16 (18, 20, 22, 24) V-sts.

Work 1 row even in patt.

Rep last 2 rows 2 times—18 (20, 22, 24, 26) V-sts.

Work even in patt until piece measures 12½ (13¼, 12½, 13½, 14)" (31.5 [33.5, 31.5, 34.5, 35.5] cm), ending with a WS row.

SHAPE ARMHOLE

Row 1: (RS) Work in patt until 3 (4, 5, 7, 8) V-sts rem, end-dec, turn leaving rem sts unworked—3 (4, 5, 7, 8) V-sts dec'd at side edge, 15 (16, 17, 17, 18) V-sts.

Row 2: (WS) Work even in patt.

Work slanted dec at end of row on RS row 1 (1, 2, 1, 2) times—1 (1, 2, 1, 2) V-sts dec'd at side edge, 14 (15, 15, 16, 16) V-sts.

Work even in patt until piece measures 17 (17¾, 17¾, 18¾, 19¾)" (43 [45, 45, 47.5, 50] cm), ending with a WS row.

SHAPE FRONT NECK

Sl st in first 9 (9, 11, 11, 11) sts, beg-dec, cont in patt to end of row, turn—5 (5, 6, 6, 6) V-sts dec'd at front edge, 9 (10, 9, 10, 10) V-sts.

Row 2: (WS) Work even in patt.

Work beg-dec at beg of row on RS row 2 times—7 (8, 7, 8, 8) V-sts.

Work even in patt until piece measures 20 (20¾, 20¾, 21¾, 22¾)" (51 [52.5, 52.5, 55, 58] cm), ending with a WS row.

SHAPE SHOULDER

Next row: (RS) Ch 2, dc in first 5 (6, 5, 6, 6) sts, hdc in next 4 (5, 4, 5, 5) sts, sc in next 4 sts, leave rem 4 sts unworked. Fasten off.

Sleeves

With larger hook and MC, ch 56 (56, 60, 64, 72).

Work even in V-st patt for 3 (3, 5, 5, 5) rows—26 (26, 28, 30, 34) V-sts on RS rows.

Inc row: (RS) Inc V-st after first V-st and before last V-st—28 (28, 30, 32, 36) V-sts.

SIZES 36 (40, 52)" ONLY:

Work even in patt for 5 (5, 3) rows. Rep inc row—30 (30, 38) V-sts.

ALL SIZES

Work even in patt until piece measures 5¼(5¼, 4¾, 4, 4½)" (13.25 [13.25, 12, 10, 11.5] cm), ending with a WS row.

SHAPE SLEEVE CAP

Note: All WS rows worked in patt.

Row 1: (RS) Sl st in first 5 (7, 9, 7, 9) sts, beg-dec, cont in patt until 3 (4, 5, 4, 5) V-sts rem, end-dec, turn leaving rem sts unworked—3 (4, 5, 4, 5) V-sts dec'd at each edge, 24 (22, 20, 24, 28) V-sts.

Row 3: (RS) Sl st in first 5 (3, 1, 3, 3) sts, beg-dec, cont in patt until 3 (2, 1, 2, 2) V-sts rem, end-dec, turn leaving rem sts unworked—3 (2, 1, 2, 2) V-sts dec'd at each edge, 18 (18, 18, 20, 24) V-sts.

Work 1 slanted dec at beg and end of row on RS rows 3 (4, 1, 1, 3) times—3 (4, 1, 1, 3) V-sts dec'd at each edge, 12 (10, 16, 18, 18) V-sts.

SIZES 44 (48, 52)" ONLY

Work 3 rows even in patt.

Work 1 slanted dec at beg and at end of row on RS row 3 (5, 3) times—3 (5, 3) V-sts dec'd at each edge, 10 (8, 12) V-sts.

ALL SIZES

Work 1 WS row in patt. Fasten off.

Appliques
BASE FLOWER

With smaller hook, ch 5, sl st in first ch to form ring.

Rnd 1: Ch 1, 12 sc in ring, sl st in first sc to join—12 sc.

Rnd 2: Ch 1, sc in first st, [ch 3, sk next st, sc in next st] 5 times, ch 3, sl st in first sc to join—6 sc, 6 ch-3 sps.

Rnd 3: (Sl st, sc, 3 hdc, sc, sl st) in each ch-3 sp around.

Rnd 4: Ch 1, BPsc (see Glossary) around first sc from Rnd 2, [ch 5, BPsc around

next sc from Rnd 2] 5 times, ch 5, sl st in first BPsc to join—6 BPsc, 6 ch-5 sps.

Rnd 5: (Sl st, sc, hdc, 3 dc, hdc, sc, sl st) in each ch-5 sp around.

Rnd 6: Ch 1, BPsc around first BPsc from Rnd 4, [ch 7, BPsc around next BPsc from Rnd 4] 5 times, ch 7, sl st in first BPsc to join—6 BPsc, 6 ch-7 sps.

Rnd 7: (Sl st, sc, 2 hdc, 5 dc, 2 hdc, sc, sl st) in each ch-7 sp. Fasten off.

FLOWER 1

Work base flower using MC1 for Rnds 1–3, CC1 for Rnds 4–5, and CC2 for Rnds 6–7.

FLOWER 2

Work base flower using CC2 for Rnds 1–3, and CC1 for Rnds 4–5. Fasten off.

FLOWER 3 (MAKE 3)

Work base flower using CC2 for Rnds 1–3. Fasten off.

LEAF (MAKE 3)

With smaller hook and CC3, ch 17.

Rnd 1: Hdc in 2nd ch from hook, dc in next 2 ch, tr in next 2 ch, dc in next 3 ch, hdc in next 2 ch, sc in next 3 ch, sl st in last 3 ch, ch 2; rotate piece to work in bottom of foundation ch, sl st in first 3 ch, sc in next 3 ch, hdc in next 2 ch, dc in next 3 ch, tr in next 2 ch, dc in next 2 ch, hdc in last ch, ch 1, sl st in tch before first hdc. Fasten off.

Finishing

With RS tog, sew shoulder and side seams. Sew sleeve seams. Sew sleeves into armholes.

SLEEVE EDGING

With RS facing and larger hook, join CC2 with sc in seam, working in opposite side of foundation ch, (ch 1, sk next ch, sc in next ch) around, ch 1, sl st in first sc to join. Fasten off.

BODY EDGING

With RS facing and larger hook, join CC2 in bottom left of front, working in opposite side of foundation ch, (ch 1, sk next ch, sc in next ch) across bottom edge, cont to work (ch 1, sc) evenly up right front edge, around neck and down left

front edge, working 2 sc in each corner, sl st in first sc to join. Fasten off.

BUTTON LOOPS

Work 3 button loops evenly spaced at right-front opening, the first at the top and the 3rd at same level as bottom of armhole, as foll: With WS facing and CC2, insert hook in ch-1 sp along front edge and pull up lp, ch 3, sl st in same sp, turn, 6 sc in 3-ch arch. Fasten off. Weave in ends securing button loop to front edge.

Sew buttons to left front opposite button loops. Sew flowers and leaves in place according to photos or personal preference. Add more flowers for larger size if desired. 🖋

ANNETTE PETAVY loves tailoring her crochet as if it were fabric. She crochets, cooks, and gardens near Lyon, France, and tells you about it on her website: annettepetavy.com.

Arc de Triomphe Cardigan

BY ANNETTE PETAVY

If you can't go to Paris, let Paris come to you with this elegant cardigan with lacy arches. Simple shaping lets the lace shine. Ours is finished with a satin bow, but you could use a classic button.

Finished Size

30¾ (38¼, 46, 53¾, 61¼)" (78 [97, 117, 136.5, 155.5] cm) bust circumference. Garment shown measures 30¾" (78 cm), modeled with 3" (7.5 cm) negative ease.

Yarn

Elann.com Peruvian Quechua (65% alpaca, 35% Tencel; 122 yd [112 m]/1¾ oz [50 g]; (**3**)): #9160 saxony teal, 7 (10, 12, 14, 16) balls.

Note: This yarn has been discontinued. Please substitute a DK weight (#3 – Light) yarn that works up to the same gauge.

Hook

Size G/6 (4 mm). Adjust hook size if necessary to obtain correct gauge.

Notions

Yarn needle; 36" (91.5 cm) of 2" (5 cm) wide satin ribbon; sewing needle and matching sewing thread.

Gauge

3 sh = 5¾" (14.5 cm) blocked; 12 rows = 5" (12.5 cm) blocked.

Stitch Guide

Shell (sh): Work 11 dc in indicated ch-5 sp.

Half sh: Work 5 dc in indicated ch-2 sp.

Lace patt (multiple of 8 sts + 1 + 1 for foundation)

Row 1: (WS) Ch 1 (does not count as a st throughout), sc in 2nd ch from hook, ch 1, sk next st, sc in next st, ch 5, sk next 3 sts, sc in next st, *ch 3, sk next 3 sts, sc in next st, ch 5, sk next 3 sts, sc in next st; rep from * to last 2 sts, ch 1, sk next st, sc in last st.

Row 2: (RS) Ch 1, sc in first sc, sh (see above) in first ch-5 sp, *sc in center ch of skipped chs of Row 1, sh in next ch-5 sp; rep from * to last sc, sc in last sc.

Row 3: (WS) Ch 3 (does not count as st), tr in first st, ch 2, sc in 4th dc of next sh, ch 3, sk next 3 dc, sc in next dc, *ch 5, sc in 4th dc of next sh, ch 3, sk next 3 dc, sc in next dc; rep from * to end, ch 2, tr in last st.

Row 4: Ch 2 (does not count as st), dc in first tr, half sh (see above) in next ch-2 sp, sc in center dc of sh 2 rows below, *sh in next ch-5 sp, sc in center dc of sh 2 rows below; rep from * to last ch-2 sp, half sh in last ch-2 sp, dc in next tr.

Row 5: Ch 1, sc in first dc, ch 1, sk next dc, sc in next dc, ch 5, sc in 4th dc of next sh, ch 3, sk next 3 dc, sc in next dc, *ch 5, sc in 4th dc of next sh, ch 3, sk next 3 dc, sc in next dc; rep from * to last half sh, ch 5, sc in 4th dc of half sh, ch 1, sc in last dc.

Row 6: Ch 1, sc in first st, sh in next ch-5 sp, *sc in center dc of sh 2 rows below, sh in next ch-5 sp; rep from * to last st, sc in last st.

Rep Rows 3–6 for patt.

Back

Ch 65 (81, 97, 113, 129). Work Rows 1–2 of lace patt (see Stitch Guide)—8 (10, 12, 14, 16) sh. Work Rows 3–6 of lace patt 5 (5, 5, 4, 4) times.

SHAPE ARMHOLE

Row 1 (dec): Sl st in first 6 sts, ch 1 (does not count as st), sc in center dc of sh, ch 1, sk next dc, sc in next dc, ch 5, sc in 4th dc of next sh, cont working Row 5 of lace patt to last sh, ch 5, sc in 4th dc of sh, ch 1, sk next dc, sc in center dc of sh, turn—7 (9, 11, 13, 15) sh.

Row 2: Work Row 6 of lace patt.

Rep Rows 1–2 of armhole shaping 1 (1, 1, 3, 5) times—6 (8, 10, 10, 10) sh. Work Rows 3–6 of lace patt 3 times. Work Rows 3–5 of lace patt.

SHAPE NECK AND SHOULDERS

Row 1: Ch 1: (does not count as st throughout) work sc in each sc, 5 sc in each ch-5 sp, and (sc, sc in center dc of sh below, sc) in each ch-3 sp to end of row—61 (81, 101, 101, 101) sc.

Mark center 29 (29, 29, 39, 39) sc for neck.

RIGHT SHOULDER

Row 2: Ch 1, sc in next 16 (26, 36, 31, 31) sc, turn.

Rep Row 2 until sc section measures ½ (½, 1, 1, ½)" (1.3 [1.3, 2.5, 2.5, 1.3] cm). Fasten off.

LEFT SHOULDER

Row 1: Sk center 29 (29, 29, 39, 39) sc, join yarn with sc in next sc, sc in next 15 (25, 35, 30, 30) sc, turn.

Cont even in sc until sc section measures ½ (½, 1, 1, ½)" (1.3 (1.3 [2.5, 2.5, 1.3] cm). Fasten off.

Left Front

Ch 33 (41, 49, 57, 65). Work Rows 1–2 of lace patt (see Stitch Guide)—4 (5, 6, 7, 8) sh. Work Rows 3–6 of lace patt 5 (5, 5, 4, 4) times. *Note: In first 3 sizes shaping for armhole and front neck beg at the same time.*

3¾ (4¾, 6¾, 5¾, 5¾)"   5¾ (5¾, 5¾, 7¾, 7¾)"
9.5 (12, 17, 14.5, 14.5) cm   14.5 (14.5, 14.5, 19.5, 19.5) cm

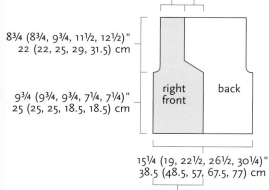

8¾ (8¾, 9¾, 11½, 12½)"
22 (22, 25, 29, 31.5) cm

9¾ (9¾, 9¾, 7¼, 7¼)"
25 (25, 25, 18.5, 18.5) cm

right front   back

15¼ (19, 22½, 26½, 30¼)"
38.5 (48.5, 57, 67.5, 77) cm

7½ (9½, 11¼, 13¼, 15)"
19 (24, 28.5, 33.5, 38) cm

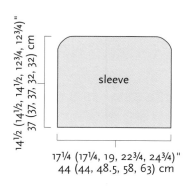

14½ (14½, 14½, 12¾, 12¾)"
37 (37, 37, 32, 32) cm

sleeve

17¼ (17¼, 19, 22¾, 24¾)"
44 (44, 48.5, 58, 63) cm

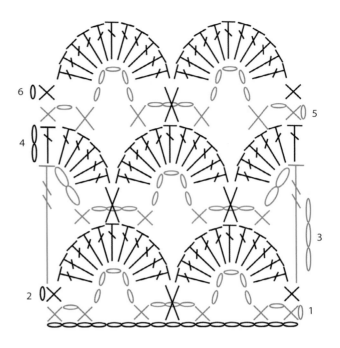

SIZE 53¾ (61¼)" ONLY
SHAPE ARMHOLE

Row 1 (dec): Sl st in first 6 sts, ch 1 (does not count as st throughout), sc in center dc of sh, ch 1, sk next dc, sc in next dc, *ch 5, sc in 4th dc of next sh, ch 3, sk next 3 dc, sc in next dc; rep from * to end, ch 2, tr in last st, turn—6½ (7½) sh.

Row 2: Work Row 4 of lace patt to last ch-5 sp, sh in next ch-5 sp, sc in last st.

Row 3 (dec): Sl st in first 6 sts, ch 1, sc in center dc of sh, ch 1, sk next dc, sc in next dc, *ch 5, sc in 4th dc of next sh, ch 3, sk next 3 dc, sc in next dc; rep from * to last half sh, ch 5, sc in 4th dc of half sh, ch 1, sc in last dc—6 (7) sh.

Row 4: Work Row 6 of lace patt.

ALL SIZES
SHAPE NECK AND ARMHOLE

Row 1 (dec): Sl st in first 6 sts, ch 1 (does not count as st), sc in center dc of sh,

ch 1, sk next dc, sc in next dc, ch 5, sc in 4th dc of next sh, cont working Row 5 of lace patt to last sh, ch 5, sc in 4th dc of sh, ch 1, sk next dc, sc in center dc of sh, turn—3 (4, 5, 5, 6) sh.

Row 2: Work Row 6 of lace patt.

Rep Rows 1–2 one (one, one, one, three) more times—2 (3, 4, 4, 3) sh.

SIZES 30¾ (38¼, 46, 53¾)" ONLY
CONT NECK SHAPING

Row 1 (dec): Work Row 3 of lace patt to last sh, ch 5, sc in 4th dc of sh, ch 1, sk next dc, sc in center dc of sh, turn—1½ (2½, 3½, 3½) sh.

Row 2: Work Row 6 of lace patt to last ch-2 sp, half sh in last ch-2 sp, dc in next tr, turn.

SIZE 53¾ (36.5 CM) ONLY

Row 3 (dec): Work Row 5 of lace patt to last sh, ch 5, sc in 4th dc of sh, ch 1, sk next dc, sc in center dc of sh, turn—3 sh.

Row 4: Work Row 6 of lace patt.

SIZES 30¾ (38¼, 46)" ONLY

Work 12 more rows even as foll:

Row 1: Work Row 5 of lace patt to last sh, ch 2, tr in last st, turn.

Row 2: Work Row 4 of lace patt to last ch-5 sp, sh in next ch-5 sp, sc in last sc, turn.

Row 3: Work Row 3 of lace patt to last sh, ch 5, sc in 4th dc of half sh, ch 1, sc in last dc, turn.

Row 4: Work Row 6 of lace patt to last ch-2 sp, half sh in last ch-2 sp, dc in next tr, turn.

Rep Rows 1–4 two more times. Rep Row 1.

SIZES 53¾ (61¼)" ONLY

Work Rows 3–6 of lace patt 2 (3) times. Work Rows 3–5 of lace patt.

ALL SIZES
SHAPE SHOULDER

Row 1: Ch 1 (does not count as st), work sc in each sc, 5 sc in each ch-5 sp, and (sc, sc in center dc of sh below, sc) in each ch-3 sp to end of row—16 (26, 36, 31, 31) sts.

Work even in sc to same measurement as back. Fasten off.

Right Front

Ch 33 (41, 49, 57, 65). Work as for left front to armhole shaping. *Note: In first 3 sizes shaping for armhole and front neck beg at the same time.*

SIZES 53¾ (61¼)" ONLY
SHAPE ARMHOLE

Row 1 (dec): Work Row 3 of lace patt to last sh, ch 5, sc in 4th dc of sh, ch 1, sk next dc, sc in center dc of sh, turn—6½ (7½) sh.

Row 2: Work Row 6 of lace patt to last ch-2 sp, sc in center dc of sh 2 rows below, half sh in last ch-2 sp, dc in next tr.

Row 3 (dec): Work Row 5 of lace patt to last sh, ch 5, sc in 4th dc of sh, ch 1, sk next dc, sc in center dc of sh, turn—6 (7) sh.

Row 4: Work Row 6 of lace patt.

ALL SIZES
SHAPE NECK AND ARMHOLE

Row 1 (dec): Sl st in first 6 sts, ch 1 (does not count as st), sc in center dc of sh, ch 1, sk next dc, sc in next dc, ch 5, sc in 4th dc of next sh, cont working Row 5 of lace patt to last sh, ch 5, sc in 4th dc of sh, ch 1, sk next dc, sc in center dc of sh, turn—3 (4, 5, 5, 6) sh.

Row 2: Work Row 6 of lace patt.

Rep Rows 1–2 one (one, one, one, three) more times—2 (3, 4, 4, 3) sh.

SIZES 30¾ (38¼, 46, 53¾)" ONLY
SHAPE NECK

Row 1 (dec): Sl st in first 6 sts, ch 1 (does not count as st), sc in center dc of sh, ch

1, sk next dc, sc in next dc, ch 5, sc in 4th dc of next sh, cont Row 3 of lace patt to end—1½ (2½, 3½, 3½) sh.

Row 2: Work Row 4 of lace patt to last ch-5 sp, sh in next ch-5 sp, sc in last sc, turn.

SIZE 53¾" (136.5 CM) ONLY

Row 3 (dec): Sl st in first 6 sts, ch 1 (does not count as st), sc in center dc of sh, ch 1, sk next dc, sc in next dc, ch 5, sc in 4th dc of next sh, cont working Row 5 of lace patt to end—3 sh.

Row 4: Work Row 6 of lace patt.

SIZES 30¾ (38¼, 46)" ONLY

Work 12 more rows even as foll:

Row 1: Work Row 3 of lace patt to last sh, ch 5, sc in 4th dc of half sh, ch 1, sc in last dc, turn.

Row 2: Work Row 6 of lace patt to last ch-2 sp, half sh in last ch-2 sp, dc in next tr, turn.

Row 3: Work Row 5 of lace patt to last sh, ch 2, tr in last st, turn.

Row 4: Work Row 4 of lace patt to last ch-5 sp, sh in next ch-5 sp, sc in last sc, turn.

Rep Rows 1–4 two more times. Rep Row 1.

SIZES 53¾ (61¼)" ONLY

Work Rows 3–6 of lace patt 2 (3) times. Work Rows 3–5 of lace patt.

ALL SIZES
SHAPE SHOULDER

Row 1: Ch 1 (does not count as a st), sc in each sc, 5 sc in each ch-5 sp, and (sc, sc in center dc of sh below, sc) in each ch-3 sp to end of row—16 (26, 36, 31, 31) sts.

Work even in sc to same measurement as back. Fasten off.

SLEEVES

Ch 73 (73, 73, 81, 113).

Rows 1–2: Work Rows 1–2 of lace patt—9 (9, 9, 10, 14) sh.

Work Rows 3–6 of lace patt 8 (8, 8, 8, 7) times.

SHAPE CAP

Row 1 (dec): Sl st in first 6 sts, ch 1 (does not count as st), sc in center dc of sh, ch 1, sk next dc, sc in next dc, ch 5, sc in 4th dc of next sh, cont working Row 5 of lace patt to last sh, ch 5, sc in 4th dc of sh, ch 1, sk next dc, sc in center dc of sh, turn—8 (8, 9, 11, 12) sh.

Row 2: Work Row 6 of lace patt.

Rep Rows 1–2 of cap shaping 1 (1, 1, 3, 5) times—7 (7, 8, 8, 7) sh.

Next row: Ch 1 (does not count as a st), sc in each sc, 5 sc in each ch-5 sp, and (sc, sc in center dc of sh below, sc) in each ch-3 sp to end of row. Fasten off.

Finishing
EDGING

At lower edge of each piece (fronts, back, and sleeves), work in rem lps of foundation ch and around ch-sps as foll: Dc in first rem lp, 11 dc in next 3-ch sp, *sk next 2 lps, dc in next lp, 11 dc in next 3-ch sp; rep from * to end of row, dc in last lp. Block pieces to measurements to open up lace patt. Sew shoulder seams. Sew sleeves to armhole. Sew side and sleeve seams.

NECK EDGING

With RS facing, join yarn to right-front lower corner, evenly sc along right front, back neck, and left front. Fasten off. Cut two 18" (45.5 cm) lengths of ribbon. With sewing needle and sewing thread, sew ribbons to fronts. 🌿

From her home near Lyon, France, ANNETTE PETAVY maintains a website atannettepetavy.com. Visit her site for blog updates, unique patterns, and crochet kits. When not crocheting or hammering on her computer keyboard, Annette is most often found in her kitchen or garden.

Abbreviations

beg	begin(s); beginning	patt(s)	pattern(s)
bet	between	pm	place marker
blo	back loop only	p	purl
CC	contrasting color	rem	remain(s); remaining
ch	chain	rep	repeat; repeating
cm	centimeter(s)	rev sc	reverse single crochet
cont	continue(s); continuing	rnd(s)	round(s)
dc	double crochet	RS	right side
dtr	double treble crochet	sc	single crochet
dec(s)('d)	decrease(s); decreasing; decreased	sk	skip
est	established	sl	slip
fdc	foundation double crochet	sl st	slip(ped) stitch
flo	front loop only	sp(s)	space(es)
foll	follows; following	st(s)	stitch(es)
fsc	foundation single crochet	tch	turning chain
g	gram(s)	tog	together
hdc	half double crochet	tr	treble crochet
inc(s)('d)	increase(s); increasing; increased	WS	wrong side
k	knit	yd	yard
lp(s)	loop(s)	yo	yarn over hook
MC	main color	*	repeat starting point
m	marker	( )	alternate measurements and/or instructions
mm	millimeter(s)	[ ]	work bracketed instructions a specified number of times

Standard Yarn Weight System

 LACE **Yarn:** Fingering, 10-count crochet thread
Gauge: 33–40 sts
Hook (metric): 1.5–2.25 mm
Hook (U.S.): 000 to 1

 SUPERFINE **Yarn:** Sock, Fingering, Baby
Gauge: 21–32 sts
Hook (metric): 2.25–3.5 mm
Hook (U.S.): B-1 to E-4

 FINE **Yarn:** Sport, Baby
Gauge: 16–20 sts
Hook (metric): 3.5–4.5 mm
Hook (U.S.): E-4 to G-7

 LIGHT **Yarn:** DK, Light Worsted
Gauge: 12–17 sts
Hook (metric): 3.5–4.5 mm
Hook (U.S.): G-7 to I-9

 MEDIUM **Yarn:** Worsted, Afghan, Aran
Gauge: 11–14 sts
Hook (metric): 5.5–6.5 mm
Hook (U.S.): I-9 to K-10½

 BULKY **Yarn:** Chunky, Craft, Rug
Gauge: 8–11 sts
Hook (metric): 6.5–9 mm
Hook (U.S.): K-10½ to M-13

 SUPER BULKY **Yarn:** Bulky, Roving
Gauge: 5–9 sts
Hook (metric): 9 mm and larger
Hook (U.S.): M-13 and larger

Crochet Gauge

To check gauge, chain 30 to 40 stitches using recommended hook size. Work in pattern stitch until piece measures at least 4" (10 cm) from foundation chain. Lay swatch on flat surface. Place a ruler over swatch and count number of stitches across and number of rows down (including fractions of stitches and rows) in 4" (10 cm). Repeat two or three times on different areas of swatch to confirm measurements. If you have more stitches and rows than called for in instructions, use a larger hook; if you have fewer, use a smaller hook. Repeat until gauge is correct.

Glossary

Learn to Crochet

Chain (ch)

Make a slipknot on hook, *yarn over and draw through loop of slipknot; repeat from * drawing yarn through last loop formed.

Slip Stitch (sl st)

*Insert hook in stitch, yarn over and draw loop through stitch and loop on hook; repeat from *.

Single Crochet (sc)

*Insert hook in stitch, yarn over and pull up loop (FIGURE 1), yarn over and draw through both loops on hook (FIGURE 2); repeat from *.

Figure 1 **Figure 2**

Half Double Crochet (hdc)

*Yarn over, insert hook in stitch, yarn over and pull up loop (3 loops on hook), yarn over (FIGURE 1) and draw through all loops on hook (FIGURE 2); repeat from *.

Figure 1 **Figure 2**

Double Crochet (dc)

*Yarn over, insert hook in stitch, yarn over and pull up loop (3 loops on hook; FIGURE 1), yarn over and draw through 2 loops (FIGURE 2), yarn over and draw through remaining 2 loops (FIGURE 3); repeat from *.

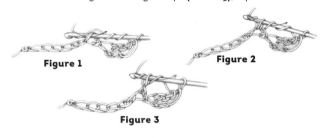

Figure 1 **Figure 2**

Figure 3

Treble Crochet (tr)

*Yarn over 2 times, insert hook in stitch, yarn over and pull up loop (4 loops on hook; FIGURE 1), yarn over and draw through 2 loops (FIGURE 2), yarn over and draw through 2 loops, yarn over and draw through remaining 2 loops (FIGURE 3); repeat from *.

Figure 1 **Figure 2**

Figure 3

Adjustable Loop

Place slipknot on hook, leaving a 4" (10 cm) tail. Wrap tail around fingers to form ring. Work stitches of first round into ring. At end of first round, pull tail to tighten ring.

Adjustable Ring

Make a large loop with the yarn (FIGURE 1). Holding the loop with your fingers, insert hook into loop and pull working yarn through loop (FIGURE 2). Yarn over hook, pull through loop on hook.

Continue to work indicated number of stitches into loop (FIGURE 3; shown in single crochet). Pull on yarn tail to close loop (FIGURE 4).

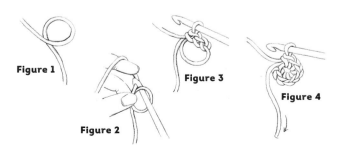

Figure 1

Figure 2

Figure 3

Figure 4

Back Loop Only (blo)

Insert the hook between the strands of the "V" and under the loop on the back side of the work. Fabric worked blo has a ridge in it and has more stretch than fabric worked otherwise. It's often used for ribbing.

Back Post Double Crochet (BPdc)

Yarn over, insert hook from back to front to back around post of stitch to be worked, yarn over and pull up loop [yarn over, draw through 2 loops on hook] 2 times.

Double Crochet Two Together (dc2tog)

[Yarn over, insert hook in next stitch, yarn over and pull up loop, yarn over and draw through 2 loops] 2 times, yarn over and draw through all loops on hook—1 stitch decreased.

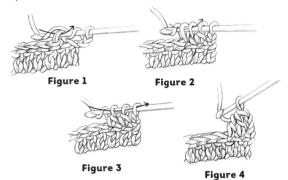

Figure 1   **Figure 2**

Figure 3   **Figure 4**

Double Crochet Three Together (dc3tog)

[Yarn over, insert hook in next stitch, yarn over and pull up loop, yarn over and draw through 2 loops] 3 times (4 loops on hook), yarn over and draw through all loops on hook—2 stitches decreased.

Double Crochet Four Together (dc4tog)

[Yarn over, insert hook in next stitch, yarn over and pull up loop, yarn over and draw through 2 loops] 4 times, yarn over, draw through all loops on hook—3 stitches decreased.

Extended Single Crochet (esc)

Insert hook in next stitch or chain, yarn over and pull up loop (2 loops on hook), yarn over and draw through 1 loop (1 chain made), yarn over and pull through 2 loops—1 esc completed.

Front Loop Only (flo)

Insert the hook under the strand of the "V" that is closest to you. Fabric worked flo is flatter and taller than fabric worked otherwise.

Foundation Single Crochet (fsc)

Ch 2 (**FIGURE 1**), insert hook in 2nd ch from hook (**FIGURE 2**), yarn over hook and draw up a loop (2 loops on hook), yarn over hook, draw yarn through first loop on hook (**FIGURE 3**), yarn over hook and draw through 2 loops on hook (**FIGURE 4**)—1 fsc made (**FIGURE 5**). *Insert hook under 2 loops of ch made at base of previous stitch (**FIGURE 6**), yarn over hook and draw up a loop (2 loops on hook), yarn over hook and draw through first loop on hook, yarn over hook and draw through 2 loops on hook (**FIGURE 7**). Repeat from * for length of foundation.

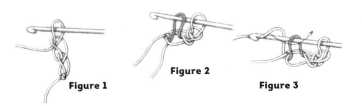

Figure 1   **Figure 2**   **Figure 3**

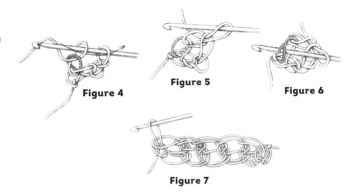

Figure 4   **Figure 5**   **Figure 6**

Figure 7

Foundation Double Crochet (fdc)

Chain 3. Yarn over, insert hook in 3rd chain from hook, yarn over and pull up loop (3 loops on hook), yarn over and draw through 1 loop (1 chain made), [yarn over and draw through 2 loops] 2 times (**FIGURE 1**)—1 foundation double crochet. Yarn over, insert hook under the 2 loops of the chain at the bottom of the stitch just made, yarn over and pull up loop (3 loops on hook) (**FIGURE 2**), yarn over and draw through 1 loop (1 chain made), [yarn over and draw through 2 loops] 2 times (**FIGURE 3**). *Yarn over, insert hook under the 2 loops of the chain at the bottom of the stitch just made (**FIGURE 4**), yarn over and pull up loop (3 loops on hook), yarn over and draw through 1 loop (1 chain made), [yarn over and draw through 2 loops] 2 times. Repeat from * (**FIGURE 5**).

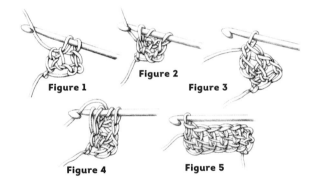

Figure 1   **Figure 2**   **Figure 3**

Figure 4   **Figure 5**

Front Post Double Crochet (FPdc)

Yarn over, insert hook from front to back to front around post of stitch to be worked, yarn over and pull up loop [yarn over and draw through 2 loops on hook] 2 times.

Front Post Double Treble (FPdtr)

Yarn over 3 times, insert hook from front to back to front around the post of the indicated stitch below, yarn over and pull up loop [yarn over, draw through 2 loops on hook] 4 times.

Front Post Single Crochet (FPsc)

Insert hook from front to back to front around the post of corresponding stitch below, yarn over and pull up loop, yarn over and draw through both loops on hook.

Front Post Treble Crochet (FPtr)

Yarn over 2 times, insert hook from front to back to front around the post of the corresponding stitch below, yarn over and pull up loop [yarn over, draw through 2 loops on hook] 3 times.

Half Double Crochet Two Together (hdc2tog)

[Yarn over, insert hook in next stitch, yarn over and pull up loop] 2 times (5 loops on hook), yarn over and draw through all loops on hook—1 stitch decreased.

Reverse Single Crochet (rev sc)

Working from left to right, insert crochet hook in an edge stitch and pull up loop, yarn over and draw this loop through the first one to join, *insert hook in next stitch to right (FIGURE 1), pull up a loop, yarn over (FIGURE 2), and draw through both loops on hook (FIGURE 3); repeat from *.

Single Crochet Two Together (sc2tog)

Insert hook into stitch and draw up a loop. Insert hook into next stitch and draw up a loop. Yarn over hook (FIGURE 1). Draw through all 3 loops on hook (FIGURES 2 AND 3).

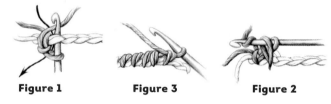

Figure 1   **Figure 3**   **Figure 2**

Single Crochet Three Together (sc3tog)

[Insert hook in next stitch, yarn over, pull loop through stitch] 3 times (4 loops on hook). Yarn over and draw yarn through all four loops on hook. Completed sc3tog—2 stitches decreased.

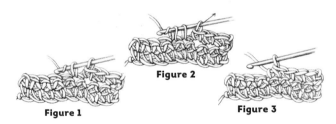

Figure 2

Figure 1   **Figure 3**

Slip-Stitch Crochet Seam

Make a slipknot with seaming yarn and place on hook. With RS of pieces facing each other, *insert hook through both pieces of fabric under the stitch loops, wrap yarn around hook to form a loop (FIGURE 1), and pull loop back through both pieces of fabric and through the loop already on hook (FIGURE 2). Repeat from *, maintaining firm, even tension.

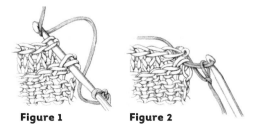

Figure 1   **Figure 2**

Stem Stitch

Bring the needle through the fabric from the back. Take a stitch as shown, keeping the thread below the needle. Repeat. The needle always emerges on the left side of the previous stitch so that the stitches overlap slightly.

Whipstitch Seam

Place pieces with right sides together. Hold pieces with the 2 edges facing you.

Step 1: Secure seaming yarn on wrong side of one piece. Pass needle through pieces from back to front at start of seam. This creates a small stitch to begin seam.

Step 2: A little farther left, pass needle through pieces, again from back to front, wrapping seam edge.

Repeat Step 2 to complete seam. Secure end of seaming yarn.

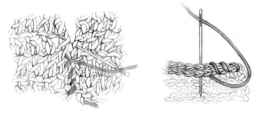

Woven Seam

Place pieces side by side on a flat surface, right sides facing you and the edges lined up row by row or stitch by stitch.

Step 1: Secure seaming yarn on wrong side of piece A at start of seam. Pass needle to right side at bottom of first stitch.

Step 2: Put needle through bottom of first stitch of piece B and pass it up to right side again at top of stitch (or in stitch above, if you're working in single crochet).

Step 3: Put needle through bottom of first stitch of piece A, exactly where you previously passed needle to right side, and bring needle to right side at top of same stitch.

Step 4: Put needle through piece B where you previously passed needle to right side, and bring needle to right side at the top of same or next stitch.

Step 5: Put the needle through piece A, where you previously passed needle to right side, and bring needle through to right side at top of stitch.

Repeat Steps 4 and 5, gently tightening seam as you go, being careful not to distort fabric. Allow rows to line up but don't make seam tighter than edges themselves. Edges will roll to the wrong side of work. Secure end of seaming yarn.

Piece A   **Piece B**

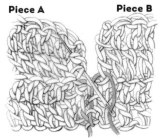

Woven seam applied "row to row"

Find popular patterns for quick and easy projects with these *Craft Tree* publications, brought to you by Interweave.

Crocheted Bags
ISBN 978-1-62033-579-6

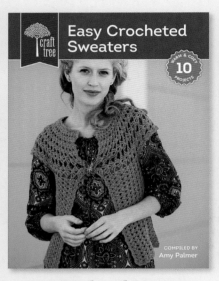

Easy Crocheted Sweaters
ISBN 978-1-62033-577-2

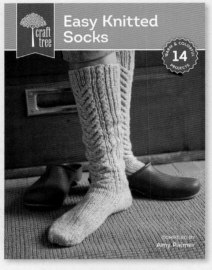

Easy Knitted Socks
ISBN 978-1-62033-574-1

Fast Crocheted Hats
ISBN 978-1-62033-578-9

Lace Knitting for Beginners
ISBN 978-1-62033-576-5

Quick Knitted Scarves
ISBN 978-1-62033-575-8

Visit your favorite retailer or order online at
interweavestore.com

 INTERWEAVE.
interweavestore.com